SEEING AND FEELING BEYOND COLORS

SEEING AND FEELING BEYOND COLORS

A PRACTICAL GUIDE TO INTERPRETING CHILDREN'S DRAWINGS

KOBY AVRAHAM

Koby Avraham (M.A.) Social Change through the Arts
Seeing and Feeling Beyond Colors
A PRACTICAL GUIDE TO INTERPRETING CHILDREN'S DRAWINGS

Published in the United States of America
Published by Spines Publishing Platform
ISBN: 979-8-90223-607-8

Spines

THE PROFESSIONAL GUIDE
TO UNDERSTANDING THE
INNER WORLDS OF CHILDREN,
ADOLESCENTS, AND FAMILIES
THROUGH DRAWING

The book was written for parents, educators, social workers, and welfare professionals (Social Services)

IMPORTANT CLARIFICATION ABOUT THE DRAWINGS IN THE BOOK

This book deals with interpreting drawings by children, adolescents, and families, a sensitive and complex field in which every line, color, and figure may reflect a rich inner world, and at times distress. Over the years, I have interpreted hundreds of drawings in therapeutic settings, parent guidance, and professional training. However, out of a deep commitment to protecting the privacy of those who drew them and to honor copyright, I chose not to use original drawings by clients or participants.

Instead, all the drawings in the book were created using AI (artificial intelligence), inspired by typical patterns observed over my years of work. They were carefully selected to illustrate emotional states, family dynamics, and common symbols in the interpretive process, while maintaining professional accuracy, ethical sensitivity, and technological innovation.

This choice is intended to allow readers to learn and deepen their understanding without harming anyone, and to ensure that the book can serve as an educational, therapeutic, and training tool in a respectful, responsible, and professional manner.

CONTENTS

INTRODUCTION: HOW DO YOU BEGIN AN INTRODUCTION TO A LIFE'S WORK? TO THE FULFILLMENT OF A DREAM?

I wish to thank whoever purchased this book and took a significant step toward understanding the field of interpreting drawings by children, adolescents, and families, a life-saving field.

Interpreting drawings by children, adolescents, and families enables parents and various professionals to get closer to the thoughts, feelings, and experiences of children, adolescents, and their family members.

Parents can gain an accurate picture of their child's inner state, including the child's personal feelings and the way they interpret reality at a given point in time, in accordance with the events occurring in their lives.

Educators will be able to apply the knowledge from the book as a regular working tool in kindergartens and schools.

Social workers may find the tools for interpreting drawings helpful for obtaining additional information about the drawers and their families, and for delving into aspects that have not yet been examined.

Welfare professionals (Social Services) will get to know children, adolescents, and families in depth, from a broad perspective. They will be able to obtain details and information that they would not have received during a regular conversation.

And to anyone who feels the need to learn about this fascinating tool.

Thank you, my personal thanks to each and every one of you.

From here, at the very opening of this special book, I extend forgiveness to the boy who sexually assaulted me at school more than five decades ago. A difficult and traumatic event that seeped deep into my life. It is what ultimately led me to this calling: to illuminate the darkness for children in the various difficult situations they endure, and to enable them and their families to receive meaningful tools to emerge from the darkness into the light.

I have forgiven you.

Thank you to my children, my grandsons, and granddaughters, who are my daily oxygen and the true reason to live on this earth.

Above all, thank you to **Michal Shelahavit-Avraham, of blessed memory**, my wife, my friend, and my great love, who passed away before her time at the age of fifty-one.

For the very privilege of living, learning, and growing stronger by her side for more than thirty years.

And thank you for the great privilege of continuing to accompany me at every step of my life.

Thank you, thank you, thank you

Koby

OPENING THE HEART AND THE BOOK: OPENING REMARKS ON ENCOUNTERING DRAWING AS AN EMOTIONAL SPACE

Drawing is a quiet, yet powerful, way to express the deepest feelings.

Through lines, colors, and symbols, toddlers, children, and adolescents share their inner world with us, even when they are not yet able to explain and describe it in words. In fact, in many cases, the person drawing is not at all aware of the information that flows from their subconscious onto the page.

This book was written to bring a professional, sensitive, and innovative perspective on interpreting drawings. To see and feel what lies beneath the surface: the feelings, fears, difficulties, and hopes that are sometimes concealed by denial or repression.

WHY DID I WRITE THIS BOOK?

As someone who was sexually assaulted in childhood at school. As someone who wrestled for years with repression and denial of the event. I know how difficult it is to give expression to such an event, especially when it is difficult to find the words.

Over twenty years of work as a lecturer and interpreter of drawings by children, adolescents, and families, I have reviewed thousands of drawings that reflected a range of emotions and experiences. Drawing is an independent medium of communication, through which the person drawing expresses themself and conveys messages.

I identified a personal and social need to establish an accessible professional infrastructure whose purpose is to help parents, educators, welfare professionals (Social Services), and social workers understand children from a new perspective, one that addresses the small details in the creation and also gives attention to the hidden layers. This infrastructure combines the development of intuition and emotional intelligence with tools acquired and learned over many years of work and practical experience.

In this book, I integrated diagnostic tools from different approaches and models I built and developed over many years of fieldwork, with the aim of creating a more reliable and complete picture of the child's inner world. And thereby allow for the construction of a precise, sensitive, and tailored treatment or guidance plan.

WHO IS THIS BOOK FOR?

- Educators, counselors, psychologists, social workers, and welfare professionals.
- Parents who wish to be involved parents and understand their children through drawing.
- Students of diagnosis, therapy, or child development.
- Any person who wants to deepen their understanding of the human soul, through understanding the symbols in drawing.

WHAT WILL YOU FIND BETWEEN THE PAGES?

- An emotional and clinical perspective for every visual component in the drawing.
- Authentic examples, professional analyses.
- Tools for creating emotional, therapeutic, or familial dialogue.
- Guidance for identifying early signs of distress, trauma, or another challenge.
- Practical guidance for emotional intervention in the educational therapeutic field.

ABOUT ME

PROFESSIONAL BACKGROUND

I research emotional development and social situations through visual symbolism. I develop therapeutic models that integrate drawing with personal, family, and social-group dynamics. I have experience writing reports for courts worldwide, and in face-to-face drawing-interpretation work with children, adolescents, and family members.

EDUCATION

- B.A. in Social Sciences – Ben-Gurion University of the Negev.
- M.A. in Social Change through the Arts – College of Society and the Arts.
- Certification in the NDFA approach for sensory regulation and developmental diagnosis (under the guidance of Rami Katz, M.A., Developmental Psychologist).
- Certification in Remedial Teaching and Learning Strategies – Achva College of Education.

PROFESSIONAL EXPERIENCE

For over two decades, I have interpreted drawings by children, adolescents, and families. During this time, I have met hundreds of families and supported children, adolescents, parents, and professionals. I teach professionals in the fields of education, welfare, and social work, and I have developed practical working methods using drawing, combining diagnostic thinking with therapeutic sensitivity.

THE FAMILY AS THE CENTER OF THE CHILD'S DEVELOPMENT

Understanding the child begins with identifying their family relationship systems. The phrase "It all begins and ends at home" expresses a concept fundamentally based on the importance of the home environment. Research shows that the family and the immediate environment significantly influence the child's development. According to Bronfenbrenner's model, the family is the closest and most influential circle, especially in the early years.

THE INFLUENCE OF ENVIRONMENT AND GENETICS

Twin and adoption studies indicate that a combination of genetic and environmental factors accounts for about 60% of the variations in intelligence, mental health, and social skills. In addition, other research findings suggest that the home environment is responsible for more than 70% of a child's initial developmental experiences in communication, emotional regulation, sense of security, and capacity for empathy.

INTERPRETING DRAWINGS AS A TOOL FOR REVEALING FAMILY REALITY

Research and experience accumulated in the field of interpreting drawings by children, adolescents, and families indicate that most of the details revealed in drawings are directly or indirectly related to the family structure and the interactions taking place within it. When children face a difficulty or challenge, it is possible to identify the sources of the difficulty and the coping mechanisms within the family framework, and at times offer solutions through it.

This approach formed the basis for developing the "Family Sits to Draw" model, which we will elaborate on in the chapter dedicated to models.

LISTENING TO THE DRAWING AND TO THE FAMILY CONTEXT

In order to identify the child's needs, pains, and challenges, it is necessary to know how to recognize the symbols and messages in the drawing. We need to understand the family context and examine the child's place within the family structure. Our role as drawing interpreters is to understand both the overt and hidden messages that the child expresses through the drawing.

HOW IS THE BOOK STRUCTURED?

In the process of gathering material for the book, a large number of drawings were collected, from which the most suitable were selected. At that time, the field of AI (artificial intelligence) was in the early stages of its development. As the collection process progressed, developments also occurred in the field of AI.

During the work on the book, two main issues arose: matters related to copyright when using drawings from external sources, and issues of confidentiality and privacy of the creators' information. After considering the relevant factors, the decision was made to use drawings created using AI, with the aim of making it easier to learn and understand the signs and the ways they are presented. In this way, the atmosphere, colors, situations, and signs are presented more clearly. In line with this approach, the material taught in this book and the way it is conveyed will enable every reader to identify and interpret a range of drawings from the realms of children, adolescents, and families in everyday life.

It is important to clarify: every AI drawing in the book was created based on an original drawing, preserving the atmosphere and the messages of the artist.

The material for the book was collected over twenty years of fieldwork. I bring you the theory, touch on research, and, above all, present the way of thinking and practice I have adopted over the years. Each chapter of the book deals with a particular topic: colors, page structure, figures, family, the tree, readiness for change, violence, sexual abuse, anxieties, and social ostracism.

In each chapter, you will find:

- Theoretical explanation.
- Analysis of visual signs.
- Clinical examples or simulations.
- Guiding questions for emotional discussion.
- Suggestions for educational or therapeutic work.

The book is written in simple, accessible language, suitable for a wide audience. It includes clear guidelines, thought and activity exercises, and recommendations for parents and professionals.

So, let's get started...

ONE

INTRODUCTION TO DRAWING INTERPRETATION AND THE STAGES OF DRAWING DEVELOPMENT

Sometimes, what a child does not say appears in the drawing space, in the space between line and color

DRAWING AS A TOOL FOR UNDERSTANDING WHAT IS HAPPENING IN A CHILD'S LIFE

Even in the early years, before acquiring speech skills, children express themselves through drawing. They convey clear ideas and messages in a comprehensible way, even in the earliest stages of drawing, including the scribbling stage.

The language of drawing develops alongside the emotional, social, and cognitive aspects, yet differs from them: it does not rely on mediation or supervision, but comes from the depths of the subconscious onto the page in the form of line, color, and free choice.

When a child creates a drawing, we can learn about the child's inner and outer worlds and the interplay between them.

By analyzing drawings, we can better understand the child's world.

WHEN WE LOOK AT A DRAWING, IT IS AN OPPORTUNITY TO ASK:

- What is the child feeling?
- What is he struggling to express?
- What strengths does he possess?
- And what is missing for him to feel secure, belonging, and seen?

The purpose of this chapter is to lay the foundations for understanding:

- What is a drawing?
- What is interpretation?
- And how does every stage in the development of drawing reflect the child's internal maturation, and his inner and outer world?

WHY INTERPRET DRAWINGS?

Interpreting drawings is a professional, complex process that helps identify distress, understand emotional patterns, and support therapeutic guidance. Through drawing, one can understand feelings, fears, family dynamics, and memories that are not always conscious.

DRAWING IS:

- A way to identify hidden emotional distress.
- A means to locate trauma or a sense of threat.
- A tool for discovering strengths, motivation, and internal resources.
- An emotional anchor that allows for starting a conversation with a child who cannot or is not ready to talk.

In work with children and adolescents, especially with those who grow up in situations of risk, vulnerability, or distress, drawing is not only a mirror, but also a real, emotional **bridge** to the person drawing.

The drawing connects the child's world to the adult's world and enables the creation of a dialogue that is not based on interrogation but on presence, trust, listening, and understanding.

THE PROCESS OF INTERPRETING DRAWINGS BY CHILDREN, ADOLESCENTS, AND FAMILIES

Parents, concerned family members, teachers, kindergarten teachers, social workers, and welfare services staff are the parties who approach the drawing interpreter.

We must **always** remember that the child who is drawing **must** have their privacy and rights protected.

Therefore, when a request is received from someone seeking an opinion on a drawing, written consent from the parents or the guardian is required. Only in exceptional and special cases will drawings be accepted for interpretation with the approval of the referring body, such as Welfare Services, Police, Family Courts, and the like.

There are several cases in which we must be especially alert to this need, to protect the child's right to privacy.

As part of the work process, the first question posed to the applicant is: "Who drew the drawing?" When it concerns a grandchild or a niece/nephew, approval from the parents is required.

In recent years, a new working method has been adopted in which, with the aim of helping the child, the drawing is accepted for review. In cases where difficulties are discovered, the response is only conveyed to the parents, or alternatively, the option of the parents contacting me for continued support will be considered.

Under no circumstances may information be given to a party that is not authorized to receive it.

INITIAL CLARIFICATIONS FOR PARENTS BEFORE BEGINNING THE INTERPRETATION PROCESS

Before beginning the process, parents must be informed about fundamental issues: **mandatory reporting** and **informed consent**.

Informed consent – this is a legal and ethical principle that obligates professionals, including physicians, psychologists, and social workers, to provide the client or guardians with a comprehensive explanation of the nature of the process, its stages, the risks involved, possible alternatives, the likelihood of success, and **the right to refuse the process**. When dealing with an adult, the explanation is given in their presence.

Mandatory reporting – In many countries, every person, and especially professionals, is obligated to report to law enforcement authorities any case of suspected harm to the health or life of a minor.

Unfortunately, this law is not implemented thoroughly. For example, in 2024, in an anonymous survey, over 70% of physicians admitted that there were cases in which they should have reported and chose, for various reasons, not to do so.

In my first meeting with the parents, I explain to them the mandatory reporting obligation that applies to me if I discover that the person drawing is at risk, and if they refuse to cooperate with providing information and treatment.

If and when this is agreed upon, I will explain the process and its stages in accordance with the principles of informed consent.

The right to privacy is important, and so is the safety of the person drawing.

INTERPRETING DRAWINGS – MAIN STAGES

The process of interpreting drawings is carried out in several stages designed to ensure an accurate, careful, and well-founded assessment of the child's condition, while strictly maintaining the child's privacy and protecting their best interests.

Initial Assessment and Request for Additional Drawings

When a random drawing is received, if a challenge, an emotional difficulty, or a concern about violence is evident, a more in-depth examination is required. At this stage, an additional drawing will be requested, and sometimes even previous drawings from the past, in order to examine whether recurring patterns, continuity, or changes in the child's condition over time are present.

Gathering Relevant Information

In any case of receiving a drawing, only basic information is required: the age of the person drawing and whether there are developmental or motor difficulties. The purpose of collecting the information is to allow an accurate understanding of the child's characteristics, without compromising confidentiality or being burdened with unnecessary information.

Recommendations and Process Summary

At the end of the examination, the parents receive a written report that includes a professional evaluation of the drawings and recommendations for further treatment. These recommendations may include my continued guidance within the process, or referral to other treatment providers, according to need and professional judgment.

INTERPRETING DRAWINGS BY CHILDREN, ADOLESCENTS, AND FAMILIES - MAIN STAGES IN THE PROCESS

1. Introductory Meeting

The process opens with an introductory meeting, held in person or online. In this meeting, the stages of the process are presented; the principles of mandatory reporting and informed consent are explained; expectations are aligned; and the process is formally opened. This stage is intended to lay a foundation of trust and transparency with the family and participants, and to ensure a full understanding of the meaning of the process and the parties' commitments.

2. Submitting Previous Drawings

A drawing serves as a mirror to the child's emotional states at the time of its creation. Therefore, it is very important to collect previous drawings, which allow identification of recurring patterns, continuity, or changes, and comparison between different times. Requesting drawings from the past helps deepen understanding of emotional processes and significant events in the child's life.

3. Submitting Drawings According to a Predefined Template

At this stage, the child is asked to draw according to a predetermined list of subjects that includes: a tree, a house, a figure (person), a family, and a self-figure. Sometimes, additional requests are added to draw a "good" animal and a "bad" animal. The instruction is given with a single word, with each drawing carried out on a separate sheet of A4 size (or larger) to expand the space for expression. Wax crayons, pastels, or a regular pencil are used, with no time limit, to allow the child freedom and personal expression.

If the child wishes to emphasize that the drawing does not represent their family, they receive a new sheet with an explicit instruction to draw their family.

4. Interpreting the Drawings

Interpreting the drawings is carried out in several stages, with the interpreter examining each drawing multiple times, hours apart, in order to identify details that were not noticed in the initial review. This stage requires concentration, patience, and mental flexibility, and makes it possible to arrive at deep insights regarding the child's emotional state.

5. Submitting Focused Drawings

During the interpretation process, if necessary, the child is asked to make an additional, focused drawing, intended to confirm or rule out a particular hypothesis. For example, when concern arises about anxiety in kindergarten, the child will be guided to draw themself in a specific activity, such as in the play corner or during lunch, to obtain targeted, relevant information.

6. Writing the Report

After collecting all the drawings and information, supplementary information is gathered from the child's parents, the educational staff, social workers, and welfare professionals. A professional impression and opinion are formulated, including recommendations for continued care. If a need for additional treatment is identified, referrals will be made only to qualified professionals. When there is a recommendation for continued cooperation, a work plan is presented that includes professional models, which will be detailed in another chapter.

MEETING TO PRESENT THE REPORT AND RECOMMENDATIONS

At the report presentation meeting, I meet with the parents, and, as needed, professional staff involved in working with the child and family.

SUPPORT AND FOLLOW-UP FOR ONE YEAR

I accompany and support the family and the professionals for an additional year, as part of my responsibility for the success of the process. However, each professional acts in accordance with their own principles.

STAGES OF DRAWING DEVELOPMENT: A MIRROR OF EMOTIONAL AND COGNITIVE DEVELOPMENT

The development of children's drawings changes over time and includes shifts in technical skills as well as emotional aspects. It is important to be familiar with the different stages of drawing development for professional purposes. Each stage indicates changes in brain development, self-perception, and the child's view of their social environment.

STAGES OF DRAWING DEVELOPMENT IN CHILDREN

Age 1-2: The Scribbling Stage

- Random drawing, without intent or control.
- Freehand movements (lines, dots).
- The child enjoys the act of drawing itself.

Age 2-4: The Advanced Scribbling Stage

- Starts to connect the movement to the result.
- Repeating "circles" and "lines" appear.
- The child may state what they are drawing, even if it is not clear to the observer.

Age 4-6: The Pre-schematic Stage

- Basic human figures appear ("head, legs").
- The drawing represents ideas, not necessarily reality.
- Details like eyes, mouth, and hands are gradually added.

Age 6-9: The Schematic Stage

- Figures become more complex.
- Details like clothes, fingers, and hair appear.
- The child begins to draw complete scenes (house, tree, sun).

Age 9-12: The Realism Stage

- An attempt to draw "like reality."
- Proportions improve.
- The use of colors is more adapted to reality.

Age 12 and up: The Observation Stage

- Awareness of perspective, shadow, and distance.
- Drawing becomes a tool for emotional and artistic expression.
- The child may compare their drawing to others and self-criticize.

Here are several example drawings; let us examine them

A 5-YEAR-OLD GIRL WHO DREW A HOUSE WITHOUT A DOOR

The drawing may hint at a sense of incapacity or an emotional blockage in relationships. In some cases, there may also be a real physical blockage. In any case, we will learn about this from additional signs. On the other hand, the absence of a door may be intentional, to tell us that something, or someone, is preventing what happens inside the house from coming out, perhaps even under duress. There is a desire to hide what is happening, to prevent, for example, relatives from entering the house, as a form of protection. The absence of a door can therefore tell us about social difficulties, fears, and anxieties. It may indicate avoidance of communication, extending to literal physical barriers.

AN 8-YEAR-OLD BOY DREW HIMSELF AS VERY SMALL IN RELATION TO HIS PARENTS.

This may point to a sense of helplessness, fear, or an experience of external control. He makes himself small in relation to others and to his family. Events are occurring around him that cause him to feel diminished. What do you think the parents' hands are telling us?

A 13-YEAR-OLD GIRL WHO DREW HERSELF AT THE CENTER OF THE DRAWING, ALONE, USING ONLY COOL COLORS

Placing the figure at the center conveys a message: I am the center of the story; I am the message, or events are happening around me. The light, faded colors can point us toward a sense of lack. They may suggest a feeling of loneliness, social alienation, or covert depression.

In this context, the family may be regarded both as a source of difficulty and as a potential solution. When a child draws, they may be expressing in their drawings experiences from their home environment, as well as interactions with parents, siblings, friends, and other figures in their lives.

Interpretation opens the door to dialogue, to questions, to a meaningful bridge.

- Where does the child feel they are positioned?
- Are there close connections or absent figures?
- Is the message they are drawing trying to

protect a family member, or is it asking to be seen?

Drawing is a language in its own right – it has logic, grammar, and meaning. Interpretation is the beginning of a process – not its end.

TWO

THE REALM OF COLORS, EMOTIONS, STATES, AND SHADOWS IN DRAWING

COLOR AS A SYMBOLIC PSYCHOLOGICAL TOOL AND A PATHWAY OF INTERNAL COMMUNICATION

"Color is the unheard voice of the soul."

WHAT IS COLOR?

A visual sensation created in our brain following an interaction between light and matter.

HOW DOES IT ACTUALLY WORK?

When light (for example, sunlight) hits an object:

- Some of the light is absorbed by the material.
- Another part is reflected from it.
- The reflected light includes specific wavelengths, which are the ones that are received by our eyes.
- The brain interprets these wavelengths **as color.**

COLOR IS ALSO A MATTER OF INTERPRETATION

The color we see depends on:

- The light source (sun, bulb, screen).
- The properties of the material (which light it reflects).
- And our brain, which interprets the information and gives it meaning.

The color the person drawing chooses for the drawing **is not random.** It reflects an emotional state, an inner experience, and a worldview. Through color, the child tells us about joy, fear, anxiety, hope, or frustration.

LET'S GET TO KNOW THE COLORS

Colors are a means of visual communication, and many have similar meanings across cultural, personal, and environmental contexts. Colors may symbolize certain emotions and qualities; for example, red is associated with energy and power, and blue is associated with calm and tranquility. Everyone who uses colors has an individual preference for choosing colors.

Look at the color swatches, try to connect to a color, emotionally. Which color feels close to your personality? Choose a color. Now, as you learn about the meanings of each color, try to see whether the color you chose actually fits the material being learned.

THE EMOTIONAL MEANING OF COLORS

We will briefly examine several common colors and their typical meanings:

- **Red**: Power, passion, sometimes anger or fear
- **Blue**: Serenity, sadness, thought, verbal ability/verbosity, nationalism, emotional distance
- **Yellow**: Joy, energy, warmth, family orientation, stress or worry
- **Green**: Calmness, growth, balance, nature, learning, sometimes jealousy or insecurity
- **Black**: Fear, sadness, threat, or a desire to hide, spatial vision, transition, and development
- **White**: Purity, cleanliness, emptiness, or a desire to hide

At the end of the chapter, you will find the **table of colors** with their meanings in various fields**.**

CASE STUDY: UNUSUAL COLORS AND THEIR MEANING – A BOY WHO DREW HIMSELF ENTIRELY IN BLACK

Background:

A ten-year-old boy, an only child in a family with emotional difficulties, the child's parents are going through a complex divorce process.

The Drawing:

- The boy drew a human figure colored in black, without facial features or any expression.
- The figure stands alone in the middle of a blank page, with no additional colors.

Analysis:

Choosing black as the figure's color points to a sense of closedness, insecurity, and fear of exposure. Black also conveys fear of the external world and a sense of threat. The absence of facial details strengthens the sense of emotional disconnection. Placing the figure at the center, alone on the page, indicates loneliness and alienation.

Family Context:

The boy feels obligated to keep a family secret that weighs on him emotionally. He feels a lack of attention and love due to the conflict between his parents.

The Therapeutic Process:

Through drawing with different colors and conversations, the boy was invited to gradually experiment with warm colors such as yellow, orange, and red, with emotional support. Role-playing and guided imagery were used to enable emotional expression, which had been blocked due to the events.

Results:

After a series of conversations and drawings, his drawings included many more colors. Colorful strokes reflected improvement in emotional expression. A more positive emotional dialogue developed with the family, and improvement in social relationships at school was reported.

TOOLS FOR CREATING CHANGE THROUGH DRAWING

Understanding the meaning of colors in children's drawings enables parents, teachers, and professionals to understand the child's inner world and to use drawing to promote processes of emotional and systemic change.

Drawing is not only a mirror of what is happening in the heart, it is also a way to touch, move, and influence; to identify emotional distress that is not expressed in words.

Repeated use of dark or dominant colors (such as black, gray, dark red) may indicate fear, sadness, stress, or a sense of danger. It is important to look not only at the color itself, but also at the quantity, the placement, and how it is used.

Opening an Emotional Dialogue Through Colors

A conversation about color choices can become a gateway to the child's emotional world:

- What did you feel when you used this color?
- Or which color would you choose right now for your mood?

Such questions help the child to talk, without feeling that he is being asked directly about their emotions.

Encouraging the Use of Colors That Promote Calm or Vitality

If the child mainly draws in cool or dark tones, you can gradually suggest that they add other hues, such as blue, green, and yellow. Not to correct, but to allow emotional variety. Sometimes the very act of offering a color is an invitation to a new emotional world.

Using Drawing to Build a Process of Change

One can suggest a series of drawings with changing color, a colorful emotional journal, or a body drawing accompanied by conversation. Changes in colors in the drawings over time may reflect genuine emotional change and provide a basis for emotional, family, or educational work.

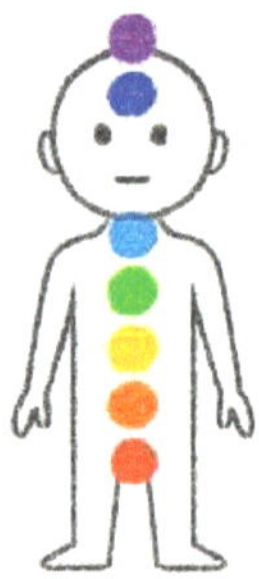

The field of colors also serves us in other domains, such as **advertising, marketing, health, and psychology.**

For example, the color chakras. Each chakra has its own color and is located in a different place in the body. Each chakra has a very precise role.

Political parties' colors are characterized by recognizable features. For example, among national parties, the dominant color is blue, while among left-wing parties, there is a preference for earth and nature tones.

The characteristics of colors hold across every field, and they play a role in conveying messages according to the color's nature or function.

MYTH-BUSTING – THE COLOR BLACK

Our acquaintance with the color black is associated mainly with darkness, fear, mourning, and difficult or negative things.

Black is also a color of spatial perception, a color of leaders, a color of transitions between dimensions.

A lot of kindergarten teachers tend to remove black from the crayon boxes to prevent the child from drawing in black. The reason is, in fact, the desire to avoid conversations with parents who ask: “Why is my child drawing in black? What is happening in the kindergarten? What is going on there? Why is my child suffering?”

Except for adolescence, in which the use of black may sometimes be linked to aspects of group identity or to emotional and psychological components, which should be examined thoroughly, black is generally perceived as a color with positive meanings. When a child chooses to draw in black, it marks a significant phase in their developmental process, representing a transition between unconscious processes and a higher consciousness in understanding reality; in other words, a symbolic process of moving from darkness to light.

TABLE 1: MEANINGS OF COLORS IN DIFFERENT FIELDS

Color	**Health/Color Psychology**	**Advertising and Marketing**	**Interpreting Children and Youth Drawings**
Red	Stimulating, increases heart rate, associated with adrenaline	Passion, urgency, energy, attention	Dominance, energy, aggression, love, need for attention
Blue	Calming, reduces anxiety, helps lower stress	Trust, security, stability, composure	Calmness, harmony, self-control, sometimes distance
Yellow	Stimulating, awakens thought, related to energy	Optimism, joy, visibility, innovation	Sensitivity, joy, intelligence, need for care
Green	Calming, signifies balance, strengthens a sense of well-being	Health, naturalness, freshness, sustainability	Growth, nature, freedom, adaptability, jealousy

Color	Health/Color Psychology	Advertising and Marketing	Interpreting Children and Youth Drawings
Orange	Stimulates appetite, evokes joy	Enthusiasm, innovation, accessibility	Energy, creativity, playfulness, optimism
Purple	Symbolizes emotional depth, encourages creative thinking	Luxury, mystery, creativity, inspiration	Imagination, intuition, spirituality, sensitivity
Pink	Calming, symbolizes warmth and security	Softness, femininity, love, romance	Tenderness, femininity, warmth, need for love
Brown	Feeling of grounding, security, connection to the earth	Naturalness, reliability, warmth	Stability, earth, security, conservatism
Black	Can symbolize depression, but also strength and confidence	Luxury, elegance, mystery, authority	Power, closedness, fear, need for control
White	Symbolizes cleanliness, calmness, a new beginning	Cleanliness, simplicity, freshness, luxury	Purity, innocence, a new beginning, emptiness

After reviewing the table, try to think of a dominant controlling color. Try to see whether the color in the advertisement suits the product or the nature of the messages conveyed in the advertisement.

EXAMPLE: THE COLOR ORANGE

Let's focus on the color orange.

According to the table, orange's characteristics are: enthusiasm, innovation, creativity, accessibility, creative energy, playfulness, and optimism. Even in the field of health, the color orange stimulates appetite and evokes joy.

The use of the color orange in advertisements by certain companies stands out in particular compared to other brands. In recent years, Mizrahi-Tefahot Bank has made consistent use of orange as a central part of its branding, with the color appearing prominently in advertising campaigns and taking a central place in the advertising drive. The bank's logo was also designed in this shade, and the messages conveyed through the campaigns include innovation, direct access to the banker, and a personal touch. Furthermore, the choice of the presenter, a comedic actor, reinforces the accessible and positive tone.

We can mention the cellular company Orange, which operated in Israel and Europe about twenty years ago. Here, too, the color orange was a central element of the branding, associated with values of innovation and a youthful, trailblazing spirit.

In a different domain, the country most closely associated with definitions of a free, innovative, liberal, and permissive state is the Netherlands. The official color of the Dutch Royal House (House of Orange), the Netherlands national football team, and the color that dominates the Netherlands as a whole is orange.

Another example, this time from healthcare, is based on experience interpreting children's drawings, over the years, in which I encountered cases that recurred several times.

Over many years, I encountered a number of cases in which the color orange indicated inflammation in the body.

One case I especially remember involved a couple who approached me to try to understand what was happening with their five-year-old boy. He could not fall asleep at night and shied away from meeting friends.

When the boy drew himself, he colored his ears bright orange. I recommended they see an ear, nose, and throat (ENT) doctor. After a medical examination, which the parents arranged, it was found that both of his ears were inflamed, which had caused his lack of sleep, the withdrawal from friends, and a fear of physical contact with his ears.

A small example of just one color.

Perform what we have just done with other colors; try to see and understand traits, processes, and behaviors through the colors and their character.

THREE

DIVISION OF THE PAGE: SPATIAL ANALYSIS IN DRAWINGS BY CHILDREN, ADOLESCENTS, AND FAMILIES

As the child positions themselves on the page, so they position themselves in the world.

SPATIAL PERCEPTION AND THE SELF-IMAGE OF THE PERSON DRAWING.

The white space of the drawing page is not just a background; it is an inner playground. Every choice the child makes, where to start, how much to fill, and where to place each detail, reflects their sense of control, self-confidence, and how they experience their place in the world.

The way the child fills the page, from edge to edge, from top to bottom, or from the sides, tells us a great deal about their self-perception, sense of security, tendency toward expansion or withdrawal, level of control, and their need for physical and emotional space.

Children who do not feel secure may "disappear" on the page, drawing small, in a corner, and avoid filling the space. By contrast, children who need control will fill the page with details, crossing lines, or frames.

A strong self-image can be expressed by drawing a large figure in the center of the page, with full details and a clear presence.

For the sake of consistency and understanding, I created and developed the following table, in which the page is divided into zones. Each zone has a different meaning, right and left, top and bottom, and the center area, which is particularly important.

TABLE 2: DIVISION OF PAGE AREAS

<table>
<tr><td rowspan="3">Introversion
Mother
Family orientation
Past
Activities within the home</td><td>Spirituality
Education from home</td><td>Imagination
Intellect
Spirituality</td><td>Goal
Future</td><td rowspan="3">Extroversion
Father
Social activities
Everything related to activities outside the home</td></tr>
<tr><td>Influence of events in the past</td><td>Ego – I
My connection to myself</td><td>Social goals</td></tr>
<tr><td>Mother
Beginning</td><td>Emotion
Instinct</td><td>Father
Roots</td></tr>
</table>

EXPLANATION OF THE TABLE: LAYOUT OF THE DRAWING PAGE - EXTROVERSION VERSUS INTROVERSION

The drawing is not only a visual expression, but also it is a living, breathing space in which every area, color, shape, and line constitutes an emotional and conscious frequency. The placement of elements on the page reflects the person's inner dynamics: between past and future, between introversion and extroversion, between mother and father, between imagination and intellect, between instinct and spirit.

The table describes two opposite yet complementary directions :

- The right side, and movement to the right, represents movement outward, to society, the future. All actions and messages related to everything that happens outside the home.
- The left side, and movement to the left**,** represents turning inward, toward the past, emotion, roots, warmth and love of, and for the family.

With an understanding of these directions, it will be easier for us to understand **pressure systems** acting on the person drawing, their intensity, and who may be exerting them. Understanding the directions of pressure is very significant in understanding the story behind the drawing: the person's difficulties, whether the pressure is personal or group-based, social, or familial.

Meanings and Connections:

The external world, the father figure represents: rules, goals, intellect, future, social functioning, formal learning, and authority. This is the Self in the public sphere.

The internal world, the mother figure represents: a sense of belonging, emotion, body, roots, past, and domestic warmth. This is the Self in the emotional, family sphere.

Extroversion is connected to movement outward, to movement toward goals, to interpersonal connections, and to experiencing the self through action and function.

Introversion is connected to emotion and internal processing, to the past, to memories, to repressed or unprocessed feelings, and to experiencing one's own existence from within.

Uses of the Table:

The table can be used in:

Decoding drawings, guidance for parents or therapists – to understand the source of the child's inner conflict, whether the child moves between an external demand for functioning and an internal emotional need.

Identifying tendencies of children and adolescents through visual or verbal expression – whether the child is drawn to action and achievement, or rather clinging to home, to the past?

Emotional processing in therapy – the drawing can reflect the tension between the extroverted and the introverted parts of their personality, or between the mother and father figures, and can highlight less balanced connections.

THE MEANING OF THE PLACEMENT OF ELEMENTS ON THE PAGE

The division is at the conceptual level; the page is divided according to more than two decades of experience in decoding drawings and dialogue with those who draw and their families.

The placement of elements can be interpreted as follows:

- Upper third of the page – imagination, thought, spirituality, hope, aspirations, ideals.
- Lower third of the page – foundation, security, need for stability, and sometimes a sense of heaviness or emotional difficulty.
- Left side – the past, relationship with the mother, inner feelings.
- Right side – the future, external connections, coping with the world, relationship with the father.
- Center of the page – the self, focal point of identity, sense of belonging to the world.

At the end of the chapter, you will find: **Table of element placement on the page.**

SIGNS OF EMOTIONAL OVERLOAD OR A NEED FOR CONTROL

A very dense drawing, with repetitive lines, fencing or encircling of the page, may indicate a need for control or a sense of threat.

An open drawing lacking a focal point may indicate emotional confusion or difficulty positioning oneself in the world.

Drawings with heavy lines at the edges, framed corners, or drawings that do not cross the page boundaries, may indicate a child who needs clear protections, or fears "taking up" space.

A very small drawing, or one that appears only in a corner, may express low self-image or a feeling of insignificance.

DRAWING INVESTIGATION CASE: A SMALL FAMILY PRESSED AGAINST THE CORNER

A SENSE OF DISCONNECTION AND LACK OF FAMILY SECURITY

Background:

A 9-year-old boy from a family of five. The parents are dealing with financial difficulties and ongoing tension at home. He is described as withdrawn and overly sensitive in social settings.

The Drawing:

The boy drew all his family members, father, mother, three children, at a very small size, placed right up against the bottom right corner of the page. There is no eye contact between the figures, and they do not touch or look at one another. The rest of the page remains completely empty, with no additional details.

Analysis:

Composition and placement: Positioning the family in the bottom right corner points to an experience of pushing the family down to a low, marginal, non-present place. The bottom right corner is often associated with a desire for change, but also with difficulty and latent fears.

Size of the figures: Drawing at a very small scale hints at a sense of worthlessness, smallness, or insignificance, both of the family as a whole in the boy's eyes, and perhaps also of his personal place within it.

Lack of eye contact: Points to emotional disconnection, distance between family members, and difficulty creating an internal dialogue. The boy may feel that although the family is "physically present," there is no real emotional connection.

Emptiness of the page: The entire page, apart from the corner, remains empty, which sharpens the sense of emotional emptiness and the absence of a "safe family space."

Family Context:

The household is under chronic stress. The parents are preoccupied with making a living and arguing about daily matters. The boy experiences the family as a closed, distant unit that does not allow emotional expression or true belonging. He may feel like a "bystander"; present physically but not emotionally.

The Therapeutic Process:

The boy was invited to gradually enlarge the family figures and to reposition each one within the space.

Wooden figures on sand were used while clarifying who is close to whom? Who is looking at whom? What would he want to happen? To encourage the creation of alternative drawings: "This is how it is now, this is how I would like it to look".

The Results:

The boy drew the family members scattered across the page space, larger, making eye contact. He described a sense of relief in being able to imagine a different reality. The combination of conversations with the child, together with the drawing work, led to a change in his perception of the family relationships.

TOOLS FOR CREATING CHANGE THROUGH DRAWING

Understanding the page space can provide us with simple, yet profound, tools for creating dialogue with the person drawing:

Emotionally Evocative Questions

- Why did you choose to draw here?
- How would you want the figure to stand if it felt more secure?
- What is missing for you in the space around you in the drawing?

Working with the Page as a Guided Space

In a meeting with the person drawing, you can ask to try drawing in the middle of the page, or to turn the page and choose a new angle, as part of a process of changing the perception of the inner space.

Creating Safe Boundaries Through Drawing

You can invite the child to sketch a line that feels to him like a boundary that protects him – a simple action that can express a need for emotional protection.

Tracking Change in the Structure of the Page Over Time

Where possible, one can compare different drawings by the child over time to understand whether he is expanding the area in which he allows himself to appear and whether his figure is growing, positioning itself at the center.

TABLE 3: DIVISION OF THE PAGE INTO LEFT AND RIGHT.

Left Side of the Page: Introversion	**Right Side of the Page: Extroversion**
Mother	Father
Domestic Activities	Social Activities
Family Ties	Everything related to outside the home
Past, Memories, Emotion, Instinct, Roots	Goal, Future, Imagination, Intellect/Mind, Spirituality
Beginning of life, Mother, Primary Emotion	Spirituality and Education away from home
Connection to self, Processing Influences	Social Goals
Inner Self	Ego — External Identity
Emotional Processing	Impact of Past Events
Mother — Acceptance, Beginning	Father — Authority, Boundaries

FOUR

THE HOUSE DRAWING: STRUCTURE, BELONGING, AND PROTECTION

Symbols and parts of the house as evidence of emotion, reality, and feelings of safety.

"The house that is drawn is not only walls and a roof, but a sense of belonging, emotional memory, and a place in the world: what is inside, what is outside, who is allowed, who is not?"

THE MEANING OF THE HOUSE

The house in drawings by children, adolescents, and adults is a central symbol that represents their inner world, sense of security, relationships, and family experience. The parts of the house in a drawing may reflect different emotional and psychological aspects.

Among children, adolescents, and in family drawings, the house reflects the sense of belonging, identity, and family connections. However, at times, more complex elements will appear, such as an emphasis on privacy, division into rooms, or highlighting certain areas in the house (for example, a personal room), in line with the development of independence and personal identity.

The house drawing embodies the child's inner relations with the family, the place where he grows up, and the emotional experience he has within the home. Every part of the house may carry meaning, both positive and negative.

WHAT HAPPENS IN AN ADULT'S HOUSE DRAWING?

Adults often experience having two homes: the childhood home, and then, once that child has grown up, a home with a sense of family belonging, with all that this implies.

What is the solution to this issue?

There are several options:

A conversation with the adult who drew the picture: "What does the house reflect? Your childhood, or your home today?"

Define the task before the drawing: "Draw your home today, or draw your childhood home."

It depends on the process we are in and the goals of that process.

There is a specific therapeutic model I developed, "Projection: From Childhood to Parenthood", which we will study in the chapter on models.

In most cultures, the house represents protection, warmth, and belonging, and at times also tension, closedness, or pain.

INTERPRETING THE PARTS OF THE HOUSE IN DRAWINGS

The House as a Whole

The house as a whole symbolizes the sense of protection, belonging, and connection to the family. A detailed house, with windows, doors, and additional elements, usually points to a sense of safety, calm, and harmony at home.

An empty house, lacking details, or one that appears unstable may hint at feelings of insecurity or emotional difficulty.

The Road/Path to the House

A path leading to the house can hint at openness, a desire for connection, and a sense of acceptance. At the same time, the path may serve to protect the house, or even as a route of escape from the house. In some cases, the absence of a path may indicate difficulty in approach or a sense of disconnection from the surroundings.

The Door

The door symbolizes openness to the world and a willingness to communicate.

A large, open door indicates emotional accessibility: "I am open to interaction with the outside society; I am open to receiving them, to hosting them in my home, in the place most important to me."

By contrast, a small or closed door, sometimes even blocked, may indicate guardedness or difficulty opening up to others. A door with a lock or a peephole can reflect a need for protection or fear of exposure.

The height and size of the handle can show how much one wants the door to be opened, or how easy it will be to reach the door. A high handle makes it harder; a low handle makes it easier to enter.

A flight of stairs before the door is a way to make it difficult for visitors. The number of steps can tell us the degree of need for protection or for a preventive approach - the more steps to climb, the harder to get there.

The Windows

The windows symbolize communication, openness, and the ability to see and be seen.

Windows may look innocent and can greatly confuse someone looking at the drawing, yet they carry a lot of information.

The number of windows, their size, their placement, (right or left, top or bottom) which window is open or closed, what is on the windowsill, what is visible from inside the house, whether there is light visible through the window, bars, the number of bars, the thickness of the bars; a window with a frame or without; a straight, sturdy window or a broken one.

The Roof

In a drawing, the roof is a symbol of the degree of protection, stability, and warmth that the child, adolescent, or family feels inside the home. The way the roof is drawn offers a glimpse into the emotional state and sense of security of the person drawing.

The Chimney

The chimney is drawn in many houses, even in places where it does not exist in the local building culture in the drawer's world. The central symbol of the chimney is communication with the world, sending messages from the house and about what happens inside it, messages that the person drawing wants to be seen as far away as possible.

How will we know how to interpret the message?

The message is conveyed through the smoke rising from the chimney, including its shape, its density, its intensity, and the direction in which the smoke is directed. The interpretation draws on sources from psychology and art therapy, which view drawings of chimneys and smoke as symbols of an emotional state and of the child's feelings toward their surroundings and home. The type, color, and form of the smoke can suggest inner feelings, relationships within the family, mood, and how the child perceives the home.

TABLE 4: SUMMARIZING TYPES OF CHIMNEY SMOKE AND THEIR INTERPRETATIONS IN CHILDREN'S DRAWINGS

Type of Smoke in Drawing	Smoke Characteristics	Common Interpretation in Child Drawing Research
White, thin, curving upwards	Delicate, lightly dispersed	Calm atmosphere, hominess, feeling of warmth and security, joy
Thick grey smoke, spreading sideways	Wide, inconsistent	Feeling of restlessness, tension, emotional confusion
Black smoke, heavy and rising sharply	Dark, straight line, emphasized	Pressure, anger, fear, worry, anxiety, or a negative experience
No smoke at all	No smoke at all	Lack of energy, feeling of emptiness or absence of warmth in the home

Type of Smoke in Drawing	Smoke Characteristics	Common Interpretation in Child Drawing Research
Smoke in atypical colors	Smoke in atypical colors	Rich imagination, active inner world, sometimes points to emotional confusion or fantasy

Elements such as size, stability, number of windows, an open or closed door, and an entry path are all symbols that carry weight in the interpretation.

TABLE 5: PARTS OF THE HOUSE AND THEIR MEANINGS.

Part of the house	General Meaning	Positive Example	Negative Example
Roof	Protection, security, parental authority, boundaries	Whole, symmetrical, colored roof-feeling of protection and emotional security	Missing, broken, or blocked roof-fear of losing control, anxieties, lack of a protective parental figure

Part of the House	General Meaning	Positive Example	Negative Example
Windows	Communication openness, connection between inner and outer worlds	Open windows with curtains- openness, communication, trust	Blocked windows, bars- difficulty in emotional expression, withdrawal, fear of emotional intrusion
Door	Access and personal boundaries	Open door in the center of the house - accessibility, balance between inside and outside	Missing or locked door- withdrawal, difficulty forming relationships, feeling of danger
Walls	Boundary and self-identity, inner strength	Thick and symmetrical walls feeling of security and differentiation	Crumbling walls - anxiety, vulnerability, emotional flooding

Part of the House	General Meaning	Positive Example	Negative Example
Rooms	Inner worlds, identity, significant figures	Labeled room ("my room," "parents' room") – self-awareness and clear identity	Confusion between rooms, a small isolated room - lack of distinction between feelings, disconnection, or emotional flooding
Smoke for the Chimney	Emotional expression, intra-family communication	Light, twisting smoke- free-flowing and released emotional dialogue	Thick, black smoke- trapped anger, fear of eruption, hidden verbal aggression
Path from the Door	Connection to the external world, emotional mobility	Clear, inviting path - feeling of security and ability to access the world	Cut-off or aggressive path - emotional disconnection, fear of the outside

Part of the House	**General Meaning**	**Positive Example**	**Negative Example**
Trees / Plants	Development, rootedness, connection to nature	Green tree with roots and leaves emotional growth, feeling of stability and belonging	Broken/withered tree - disconnection from roots (family/past), trauma, or emotional delay
Sun / Sky	Mood, hope, spirituality	Sun shining in blue sky - optimism, connection	Rain, grey sky, disappearing sun - sadness, depression, feeling of distance

EXAMPLE DRAWING ANALYSIS: LARGE HOUSE WITH WALLS AND A CLOSED DOOR – EMOTIONAL DISTANCE IN A SUPPORTIVE ENVIRONMENT

Background:

An 8-year-old boy, the eldest in a well-groomed family that appears perfect on the outside. The parents are very involved, defining themselves as warm and supportive, but they find it difficult to hear negative emotions from the child. There is no history of overt trauma, but there is a tendency to avoid dealing with pain.

The Drawing:

The child drew a very large house that takes up almost the entire page. Around the house are high walls, and the main door is sealed shut; the figure representing the child does not appear. The child says it is standing far from the house, in the corner of the page.

Analysis:

Composition: The central house, enormous in size, creates a sense of threat and frames an experience of alienation and a diminished sense of self in the face of a system that feels too big.

High walls: symbolize overprotection or an emotional barrier, sometimes out of a wish not to expose pain, or as an unconscious mechanism by the parental figures to keep threatening feelings at bay.

Closed door: a communicative blockage. The child experiences emotional rigidity, difficulty approaching the significant figures, even if there is physical access.

Absence of windows: underscores the absence of communication or the possibility to see and be seen, indicating difficulty in receiving and offering emotional expression.

The gap between the drawing and reality: the child's experience is subjective, although the parents see themselves as supportive, the child may feel they must hide parts of themselves in order to be accepted, creating a deep and confusing sense of distance.

Family Context:

The family is careful about proper appearance and correct conduct. Negative feelings such as sadness, anger, or frustration are rejected or silenced, at times unconsciously. The child feels there is no room to be vulnerable, and therefore distances themselves emotionally despite the supportive physical presence.

The Therapeutic Process:

The child was invited to draw a house that one can enter and to imagine what is inside. Games were integrated, and an indirect dialogue was conducted with the parents about the possibility of hearing unpleasant emotions without fixing or being alarmed.

The Results:

In later drawings, open doors appeared, a path from the door to the child's figure, and lit windows. The figure itself grew and moved closer to the house. The child began to express disappointment to the parents (calmly) and reported feeling truly seen. The parents described a process of personal learning to be less perfect and more present.

EXPLORING A SAMPLE DRAWING - THE CHILD SITS ALONE ON A SMALL BALCONY, SEARCHING FOR PRIVACY WITHIN A CLOSED FAMILY SPACE

Background:

A 9-year-old boy, the middle child in a family of three children. The parents are involved but very busy, and the home is described by the child as noisy, with a lot of mess. The child is characterized by high sensitivity and a tendency toward introversion, and struggles to find a quiet space for himself.

The Drawing:

The child is sitting on a small balcony, alone beside potted plants. The other family members do not appear in the drawing.

Analysis:

The balcony as an intermediate space: The balcony represents a place "between inside and outside" not inside the house (the crowded family space), and not outside it (the social world). It is the child's symbolic proposal for resolving the tension between the desire for connection and the need for protection and quiet.

Sitting alone: points to a strong need for privacy, internal processing, and an emotional space.

This is an emotional refuge.

The choice to place himself there symbolizes a need to control boundaries and to be in a place where he is not required to function in relation to others.

The absence of connection with figures: strengthens an experience of emotional differentiation, not necessarily alienation, but a need for a break from ongoing, perhaps overwhelming, contact.

The Family Context:

This child is subject to sensory and emotional overload at home, even if the parents are loving and present. He does not have a quiet corner that meets his need for emotional privacy. At times, he is asked to be with everyone, even when he needs quiet for himself.

The Therapeutic Process:

The drawing served as a starting point for a dialogue about the balcony: "What is on it? Why did he choose to sit there? What helps him feel safe?"

The parents helped the child create a concrete space of quiet and choice, physical and emotional, without viewing it as withdrawal.

The Results:

The child began to draw himself inside the house, but next to an open window or a defined corner. He feels more comfortable when allowed a moment alone. The parents learned to stop getting anxious about him, sometimes isolating themselves, and that reduced the pressure on him as well.

FIVE

THE TREE DRAWING: ROOTS, TRUNK, AND CANOPY IN EMOTIONAL TIME

The tree is a tool for information about events and growth processes, with reference to the past, present, and future.

"The tree in the child's drawing is a reflection of the soul, in every trunk, branch, and crack, lies a clue to the inner world and the developmental journey they are undergoing."

The tree is an extensive source of information in the field of interpreting children's drawings; it also gives us information across a wide range of time frames. The tree provides us with information that comes from the past, the present, and even information about the future, or, more precisely, future potential.

Over the years, I have noticed a connection between the structure of the tree's branches and the structure of the brain. We will elaborate on this later, in learning about the tree in the interpretation of children's and adolescents' drawings.

EVENTS THROUGHOUT THE LIFE OF THE PERSON DRAWING

The tree unfolds events across the entire life of the person being drawn. The entire length of the tree, from the tip of its roots to its highest point, represents the life span of the person, drawing up to the time of the drawing. It does not matter how old the person drawing is, whether five, ten, or fifty. It also does not matter how large the tree is in the drawing.

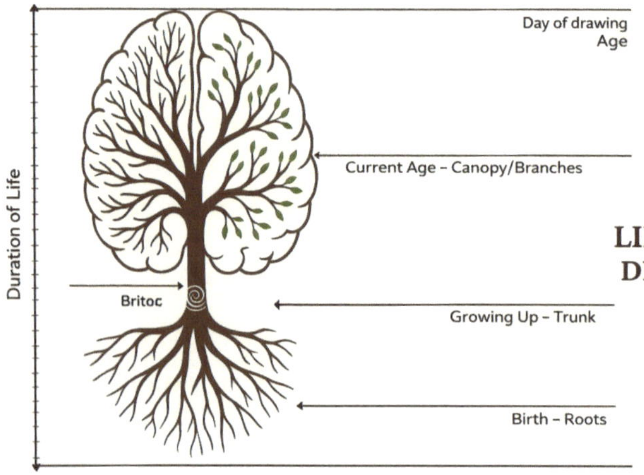

LIFE TREE DRAWING

The beginning of the roots, or the trunk if there are no roots, is essentially the date of birth of the person drawing. The tip of the tree's canopy is the age of the person drawing on the day the drawing is made.

The length of a tree from its beginning to its end is effectively equivalent to the age of the person drawing, and the course of their life...

With this information, we can, in effect, place a timeline ruler alongside the tree, divided into years, months, and days. We can look at an event in the drawing at the point in time when the event occurred. We can understand whether the event affected the person drawing, and for how long.

THE WOUND IN THE TREE: SPIRAL OR HOLE

A wound in the form of a spiral, or a hole in the trunk, recurs in many drawings.

- The wound may represent an unresolved emotional injury.
- It may be related to a childhood memory, trauma, or an emotional place the child cannot close.

At times, it appears without the child being able to explain why, the wound's size indicates the duration of the crisis or event.

Since we know the age of the person drawing, and can place the age ruler along the length of the tree, we can determine at what age the event began and at what age it ended.

STUMP, A BROKEN BRANCH ON THE TREE

When one of the branches is broken, within the landscape of a whole tree, this can symbolize a specific event, perhaps a quarrel or a conflict. When a tree has many broken branches, the story is entirely different; it can indicate chaos, at times ongoing violence, and, in certain branch shapes, sexual violence as well.

THE TREE IN THE DRAWING AS A JOURNEY THROUGH TIME:

- **Roots – the past**, the place the child comes from, past experiences, and memories.
- **The trunk – the present**, the current sense of self, stability or instability.
- **The branches – the future**, growth, aspirations, and connections that are being built going forward.

- **The leaves / fruits / flowers** – realization of potential.

THE TREE AND KEY SYMBOLS OF PERSONAL AND FAMILY DEVELOPMENT:

- A tree with deep, prominent roots – a sense of belonging and connection to the past.
- A tree without roots – at times a sense of detachment, difficulty taking hold, or a shaken identity.
- A stable, thick trunk – self-confidence, stability, and resilience.
- A thin or leaning trunk – difficulty withstanding pressure, vulnerability, excessive flexibility.
- Numerous branches that split – suggest internal space, curiosity, and personal development.
- Broken or folded branches – experiences of loss, vulnerability, or processes that were cut short.

These dimensions make it possible to see in the drawing not only an emotional state but also a life course.

CASE STUDY - THE BARE TREE

Case Description:

As part of my work with a youth group, in a unique project I initiated, Pencils of Hope, they were asked to draw a tree. One of them drew my particular attention: the bare tree.

A 17-year-old adolescent, in advanced stages and tests for his enlistment in the military.

The state of the tree drew my attention; I spoke with the adolescent, and here is the case description.

The Drawing:

A dry tree, without leaves, with roots above the ground. The trunk in the shape of an S draws special attention; we will address the S later. We can see the dimensions of the large tree spanning the entire drawing page, with the S at the center of the drawing. Above it is the dry crown, and below it the roots that are above the ground; the ground, in fact, does not exist. What does this mean?

Let us return for a moment to reality and ask: when is a tree dry, without leaves? When it has no water, it dries out. When do all the roots appear above the soil? When the tree has been uprooted. These are two natural processes that we use in our interpretation of the drawing.

Let's get back to the analysis of the drawing itself...

When I look at the drawing, after an overall look at it, I begin to search for hidden signs, ones that may rise from the subconscious, ones that sometimes even the person drawing is not really aware are there.

Because of the trunk's unique S shape, I began to look for messages in that area.

Note the two circles I added to the drawing, are you able to make out birds? Maybe the head of a hawk or an eagle?

We will gather this information as well for the ongoing analysis.

Let's look at this marking, what can you see there?

Can you see the letter "Shin" on the mezuzah (a sacred object in Judaism affixed to the doorposts of Jewish homes, invoking God's protection and blessing over the home and its inhabitants)? The letter Shin on the mezuzah represents "Guardian of the Doorways of Israel"?

So, we have here three signs taken from everyday life, from nature. One sign is also linked to Jewish culture. We will return to this later...

Let's now focus on additional information, the conversation with the adolescent...

The Conversation with the Adolescent

When I saw the drawing, I approached the adolescent who drew it and created a positive, quiet, comfortable space for conversation. Just before the conversation, *I asked for permission* to jot down a few notes from our talk. If he preferred that I do not, also paying attention to body language, then *I let go* of that need. We began to talk, starting with *general* questions (How are you? How is your week going? Which soccer team do you support?), then *rapport-building* ones (amazing shirt, where's it from? I have one like that too), aimed at creating a safe space for the adolescent so he could continue in an open, collaborative way.

Gradually, I moved on to the drawing itself. By the way, this can take time; it can also wait until the next session to dive in. We need to be sensitive to the adolescent's responses, emotional, physical, and body language.

In the conversation, just as here, I separate the parts of the tree and focus for a few minutes on each area. Depending on his age, I also show what I marked here. Do you see the birds? Do you see the letter S? Do you see that there's a symbol from the mezuzah here?

I try to understand from him: Why are there no leaves on the tree? Why did he draw in pencil? If possible, we begin to use *personification*: Does something in you identify with the tree? Is the tree sad? Is the tree hot? After each question, I give the adolescent time and space to think, connect emotionally, build confidence, and, of course, I do not interrupt him as he thinks and expresses himself.

Data Collection

At this stage, we have the drawing and the conversation with the adolescent. If there is a sense that something deeper is present, I may turn to additional sources, such as the school counselor, one of the parents, or any other authorized party.

When writing the conclusions and recommendations, I integrate all the information available in order to build the correct tool for moving forward.

It is important to note that I *always* separate the analysis of the drawing and its interpretation and the additional information I receive. Even before the conversation with the adolescent, I already had my interpretation of the drawing. I use the additional information to examine and refine the direction I already have.

The Story of the Drawing – The Bare Tree

These are days of war in Israel; this is reflected in this very distinctive drawing.

The adolescent who is about to be drafted into the IDF (Israel Defense Forces) expresses anxiety, fear, and hopelessness about the future. The roots and trunk of the tree are not connected to the ground; there is no grip on the soil. In fact, there is no solid ground under his feet, no stability. The tree's crown, which is supposed to forecast future potential and teach us about the abilities of the person who drew it, is completely dry. There is absolutely no life. And at the center of the tree, the letter S represents a powerful confrontation between two conflicting sides. The confrontation can be read as personal, ideological, national, and of course, military. Even the tree's overall shape reminds us of a snake, the fear of a bite.

At the top of the tree, the place of spirit and faith, right in the center, on the "forehead", the letter Shin from the mezuzah symbol.

In my view, the adolescent is already beyond expressing worries; he is already in an anxious state influenced by everything he sees, feels, believes, and experiences in his life.

My recommendation was to include the adolescent in a support group with young people facing similar challenges, and in parallel, or alternatively, to begin sessions with a therapist, with an emphasis on working together with the parents.

Important to remember, all the processes I present here in the book are worth learning, along with the guiding principles of the approach. The action is the same action, the approach is the same approach. The data changes, but the approach remains the same.

During my academic studies, one lecturer gave me an example of this. 1+1=2 is exactly like 2+2=4, and like 3+3=6. When he prepared us for the exam, he asked us to solve the same five exercises over and over so that the brain would build the approach itself into memory.

THE LINK BETWEEN THE TREE AND THE STRUCTURE OF THE BRAIN - TREE-BRANCHES MODEL AS A REFLECTION OF HEMISPHERIC BRAIN FUNCTION

The human brain is divided into two hemispheres, right and left. Each hemisphere is divided into four lobes, but the main division is into two hemispheres. Each one specializes in processing different kinds of information. *The right hemisphere* is responsible for *creative, intuitive thinking, imaginative spaces, music, and holistic perception. The left hemisphere* is responsible for *logical, verbal, mathematical, and analytical* processes. On this basis, I developed this model of *the analogy between the tree and the structure of the brain.*

When we look at children's drawings, we can identify whether the person drawing is more logical and analytical (left hemisphere) or more creative, intuitive, and emotional (right hemisphere), through the drawing style, the organization of the page, and the visual language.

THE LEFT HEMISPHERE – LOGICAL, ANALYTICAL THINKING

In a drawing that reflects left-hemisphere dominance, one can discern straight lines and geometric structures that indicate a tendency toward order, precision, and symmetry. Additional characteristics include the presence of small, precise, meticulous details, reflecting attention to fine points and breaking components down into small parts. Sometimes numbers are integrated into the drawing, such as house numbers or quantities, as part of how analytical thinking manifests. The result is a drawing characterized by order, careful planning, and great precision in the details.

THE RIGHT HEMISPHERE – CREATIVITY, INTUITION, AND EMOTIONAL EXPRESSION

In a drawing that reflects right-hemisphere dominance, we will see many more colors and shades, more rounded, dynamic lines. More figures will appear, most of which express emotion. We will also see a drawing with extensive use of visual symbols that relate to or express feeling, such as hearts, a sun smiling at the world. Overall, the drawing will appear *less orderly* to the eye in terms of structure.

APPLICATION AND BENEFITS

After interpreting hundreds of tree drawings over the past twenty years, and conversations with educators, parents, and social workers, one can see a correspondence between the number of branches, their density on a certain side of the tree, and various strengths in the logical or visual domain. We will now see several explanatory examples.

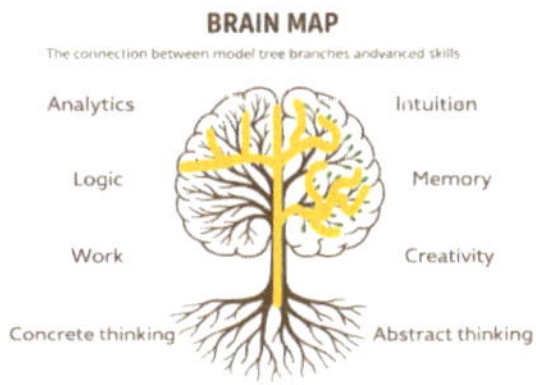

There are several advantages when one knows how to examine these data: *professional guidance can be given for continued studies*, and it is possible to check *where there is a particular weakness that can be strengthened* with appropriate physical activity or intensified learning. One can identify *where there are obstacles or difficulties in developing processes*, such as taking a process from its start to finish, achieving the desired results, or implementation a particular process.

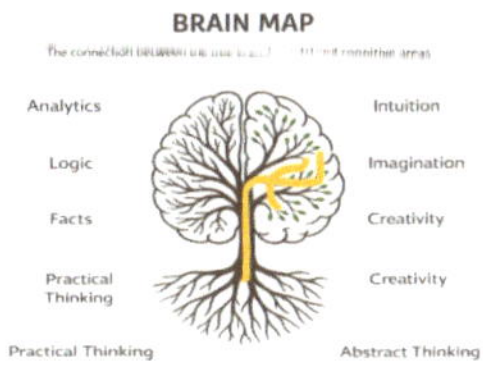

The model I developed offers a visual and diagnostic representation of hemispheric activity through the image of a tree and its branches.

According to this model:

- The form of the branches and their density in different areas of the tree reflect the degree of activity and strength of each brain hemisphere.

- Areas with many branches express active brain domains, with strong, well-established functioning.
- Areas sparse in branches point to functional weakness or unrealized potential in the corresponding brain hemisphere.

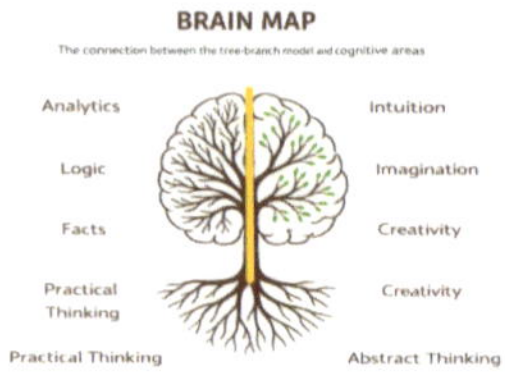

Using this model, one can identify difficulties in crossing the midline. Strengthening the connections between the two hemispheres leads to improved memory retrieval and a significant improvement in learning abilities.

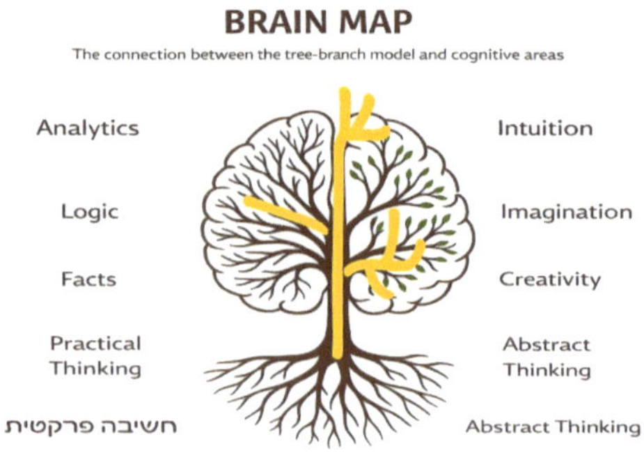

VARIOUS SIGNS WORTH KNOWING

- *Thick trunk at its base*, indicates stability and grounding. At times, one can see changes in trunk thickness (widening and narrowing several times) from which we can learn about shifts in the intensity of the person drawing over the years.
- *Thin trunk*, indicates weakness and lack of stability; at times, this may be a physical weakness, and at times, an emotional or mental weakness.
- *A very large tree*, may indicate a need to be seen, or a well-developed ego. Alternatively, it can signify a search for meaning.
- *A small, compact tree*, sometimes represents avoidance, shyness, or a sense of low self-worth.
- *Dark, thick, or turbulent soil*, emotional distress, unsafe foundation.
- *Absence of ground/soil*, detachment from reality, difficulty feeling protected.
- *Branches reaching upward*, aspiration and growth.
- *Branches drooping downward*, a sense of heaviness, fatigue, or loss of hope.

SIX

THE HUMAN FIGURE IN DRAWING: BODY PARTS, EXPRESSION, AND THE EMOTIONAL ANATOMY OF THE DRAWN PERSON

"The figure drawn on the page is not just a body; it is a representation of identity, self-worth, and a reciprocal relationship with the drawer's world."

WHY START WITH A FIGURE RATHER THAN A FAMILY?

The chapter on interpreting the human figure is studied just before the interpretation of family drawings. Essentially, the family is a group composed of several figures, so we need to understand the figures and their signs before we begin to interpret relationships between figures.

One of the best-known projective tests in developmental and clinical psychology is the **Draw A Person (DAP) test**.

All the elements examined in this test for the figure are, in practice, exactly the same elements that are examined when we interpret a figure drawing in the analysis of children's and adolescents' drawings.

The test is used to assess cognitive development, self-image, emotional distress and trauma, and interpersonal difficulties in relationships and social contexts.

PRIMARY SIGNIFICANCE:

A figure drawing reflects how the child perceives the figure: *their feelings toward it, the intensity of the connection* or the *distance*, and the *characteristics which they attribute to it.*

In a figure drawing, the child projects their inner world, *fears*, *wishes*, *conflicts*, onto the drawn figure, while also revealing their view of its role, status, and influence on them.

WHAT DO WE EXAMINE WHEN ANALYZING THE FIGURE DRAWING?

- **Body proportions** – Are the figure's proportions, the size and relationship of the limbs, balanced? For example, did the child draw a very small head on a large body?
- **Presence of body parts** – We check the presence of all parts, e.g., limbs. *Missing parts* can inform us about a *physical limitation. Missing hands* can indicate difficulty, possibly suggesting helplessness. *Missing legs* or feet may suggest limitations in physical and emotional movement.

- **Emphasis on body parts** – When parts such as the *mouth* or *hands* are emphasized, this may indicate emotional difficulty or conflict; these two elements can also guide us to consider the possibility of sexual abuse.
- **Pressure and line intensity** – Reflecting muscle tone, the shoulder girdle, and the wrist. When we see a *very strong line*, it may hint at *anxiety* or express *frustration*. If the *line is weak*, it may indicate *insecurity* or *physical fatigue* in the person drawing.
- **Additions to the figure** – When accessories or extra parts are added to the standard figure, we may learn about a desire to hide oneself (dark sunglasses) or to conceal physical injury to the body (excessive clothing). In many cases of drawings related to sexual violence, we may notice the addition or exposure of male or female genitalia.

When exposed organs are concealed by clothing yet still visible, this serves as a hint or a strong reinforcing sign of the possibility of sexual abuse.

- **Placement of the figure on the page** – suggests the person drawing's sense of their place in the larger world and in their family or social life.
- **Facial expressions** – Facial expressions are clear indicators of emotional expression, *fear and anxiety, joy and success, sadness and failure*. Each such emotion is clearly reflected in the facial features.

In a portrait drawing, when an emotional expression appears through the depiction of the face, it may sometimes contradict *the way the rest of the figure was drawn.* This contrast may add depth, complexity, and even multiple meanings to the messages.

BODY PARTS AND THE CONNECTION BETWEEN EMOTION AND REASON

My explanation of the figure will be divided according to the different body regions.

Upper Torso

This part includes *the chest*, the center of which is *the heart*. Everything related to *emotion, feelings of love, and blood flow*. We continue upward, where *the neck* is located, and above the neck are *the head, the brain,* the cognitive capacity to process data, weigh considerations, and make decisions, *it's all in the head*. It is no accident that we often mention the phrase "it's all in the head" when describing a person's difficulties. Negative emotions, fears and anxieties, repressions and denials, *it's all in the head*.

The Neck

The neck is essentially *the connecting link* between *emotion and the heart and reason*. In practice, we face the need to decide and choose between what *the heart feels* and what *reason advises us*, even in simple day-to-day actions.

Sometimes we see drawings *where the head is attached to the shoulders without a neck*, and sometimes the neck is *very long and thin*. Sometimes the neck is *very thick*. What might all this teach us about the conscience of the person drawing? About the ability to separate emotion from intellect? About their decision-making ability?

The means of communication for *receiving* information (eyes, ears, nose) are located close to the brain and reason, as is the organ for *delivering* information (the mouth). This is the area where we make decisions rationally.

By contrast, these organs are *distant from the heart*, which is the source of emotion.

The Ears

The ears are the organ of *hearing*, the organ of *listening*: “I hear the other”. When children and adolescents draw a head, they sometimes draw it without ears. What are they trying to say? "I'm not listening," perhaps ignoring? Or maybe “no one is listening to me?”

What about the *size* of the ear?

Large ears are a sign that “I am curious; wanting to hear from farther away?” Or perhaps, “I am afraid, I am worried, and therefore my ears are large; I am heightening my alertness”, just as a dog lifts its ears when it hears a rustle or senses danger?

What About the Eyes?

I have no eyes, or enlarged pupils, blacked out or missing, which could mean "I do not want to see anything?" Or maybe "no one sees me at all". What about the pupils? Black eyes, hollow eyes, perhaps I am witnessing events that *I would prefer not to see?*

The Mouth and the Lips

The organ of speech, the organ of love and sensuality. If I do not have a mouth, does that mean *I cannot* speak? Maybe I don't have the strength to speak? Am I being prevented from speaking? Am I unable to express love? Sensuality?

Emphasized lips and a large mouth can point to high verbal expressiveness, at times even obsessive; in quite a few cases, to overexposure to sex, and in special cases even to sexual coercion.

The Nose

The sense of smell: people tend not to regard the nose as a communicative organ, even though the sense of smell governs many areas connected to emotion, memories, fears, anxieties, love, and sexuality. The sense of smell has an additional, highly significant dimension that also affects how we behave in society.

Like the other senses, the sense of smell can be in states of excess or deficiency, concepts related to the regulation of the sensory system. An imbalance in this system markedly affects our behavior as adults, all the more so when dealing with children.

A drawing of a nose, in its size, shape, and emphasis, can serve as a tool for projecting visual signs related to the regulation of the sense of smell and help identify behavioral difficulties. A large nose indicates difficulty with a certain smell; perhaps the person drawing is sensitive to a smell present in a particular place? "*I do not want to go* to a certain place because the smell repulses me."

The person drawing changes their behavior because of a smell, and is even willing to *use physical force* in order not to endure the terrible smell. We will discuss this in a case study at the end of the chapter.

THE LOWER BODY FROM THE CHEST DOWNWARD

The Hands

The hands are a body part that can symbolize gentleness, strength, physical power, or the expression of loving emotions.

The structure of the hands, their visual form, and their proportions relative to the size of the body are important. One hand long, one short, *Long Arm Syndrome is an indicator of recurrent abuse. We* will elaborate on this in the chapter on sexual violence.

The Feet

The feet represent the ability to move and the direction of movement. Are both feet pointing in one direction? Are the feet pointing in opposite directions? What are the differences in size between one foot and the other? This has great significance when we interpret the drawn figure.

In drawings by children, adolescents, and families that deal with physical and sexual violence, the very form of exposure and the manner in which it is depicted are important.

If the body is naked, this may carry a certain interpretation not necessarily of coercion. It is possible that the child is growing up in a family that allows exposure of genitals, such as shared showers, or even walking around the home naked.

Also, exposure to body parts can occur through erotic films, which can be easily found across the internet.

The following table describes various body parts and their possible interpretation when they are reduced in size or enlarged and emphasized.

TABLE 6: REDUCED OR ENLARGED AND EMPHASIZED BODY PARTS AND THEIR POSSIBLE INTERPRETATION

Body Part	Meaning When Enlarged	Meaning When Reduced	Additional Examples/Notes
Head	High intellectual estimation, emphasized imagination, grandiosity, ambition for leadership or control	Lack of self-confidence, feeling of smallness, avoidance of thinking, or weakness	A giant head can indicate "big-headedness" in the family/class
Eyes	Need to see and observe, hyper-vigilance, anxiety, curiosity	Desire not to see, closed-off nature, anxiety, hiding emotions	Hollow/erased eyes — a symbol of deep distress

Body Part	Meaning When Enlarged	Meaning When Reduced	Additional Examples/Notes
Mouth	Need to express emotions, preoccupation with words or eating, impulses	Difficulty in self-expression, silence, fear of exposure	Erased mouth — sometimes a sign of a secret, shyness, or verbal trauma
Hands	Need to act, control, sometimes aggression, expression of power	Helplessness, difficulty acting, concealment, shyness	Large hands — desire "to influence the world"
Legs	Search for stability, security, presence in the world, independence	Lack of self-confidence, detachment, difficulty holding onto reality	Legs in the air — a feeling of "floating" or detachment
Shoulders	Shoulders Pride, physical strength, resilience, confronting difficulty	Sensitivity, lack of resilience, weakness	Wide shoulders — masculine image or protection, sometimes physical and

Body Part	Meaning When Enlarged	Meaning When Reduced	Additional Examples/Notes
			sexual aggression
Belly /Waist	Emotional tension, preoccupation with the body, internal conflict	Physical weakness, difficulty coping with impulses	Thick waist — need for protection/ authority
Hair	Preoccupation with appearance, sexuality, gender identity	Feeling of weakness, low self-worth, concealment	Unusual hair — emphasis on gender image or individuality
Ears	Sensitivity to criticism, need to listen	Closed-off nature, difficulty opening up, non-listening	Large ears — hyper-vigilance, or anxiety
Breasts/ Chest	Preoccupation with sexuality/gender identity, need for attention	Discomfort with the body, concealment, or denial	Chest emphasizes femininity or masculinity, depending on the background

TABLE 7: THE FIGURE AND POSSIBLE MEANINGS

Feature	Possible Meaning
Size of the Figure	**Large figure** — need for control or strong self-expression **Small figure** — low self-image or a feeling of invisibility
Placement on the Page	**Center of the page** — confidence **Corner or margins** — feeling of detachment or anxiety
Missing Limbs/Parts	**Missing hands** — difficult connecting or a feeling of helplessness **Missing mouth** — fear of speaking or a repressed secret
Eyes	**Large eyes** — need to see and be seen Eyes without pupils — fear of reality or trauma
Line Pressure	**Strong line** — powerful emotional expression or tension **Weak line** — sensitivity, hesitation, or emotional suppression
Exaggerated Details	Emphasis on a specific part (e.g., teeth, fingers) may indicate anxiety, aggression, or focal trauma

USES IN SOCIAL WORK

- *Initial emotional assessment* – A non-invasive tool that enables initial contact with the child.
- *Monitoring a therapeutic process* – Drawings over time reveal changes and prolonged inner processes. This is a tool that can be examined over the years.
- *Indirect dialogue with the child* – Through the figure they drew, you can ask questions such as "What is their name?" "What are they feeling?" and open a safe emotional dialogue.
- *Understanding family dynamics* – Combining a figure drawing with a family or house drawing can deepen the information the social worker receives about the family as a whole.

PRACTICE EXERCISE - WHERE DOES THE FIGURE FEEL SAFE?

- Exercise objective: to reveal the child's feeling of internal positioning within an emotional space, through the figure's placement in the drawing and its relationship with the space of the page.

STAGES OF THE EXERCISE

Open Invitation:

Ask gently:

"If you were to draw a figure, where on the page would you like to draw it?"

Choice and Execution:

The child draws a single figure in the place they chose on the page.

Encourage complete freedom, without corrections or criticism.

Emotional Reflection:

Possible Questions:

- What does this figure see around it?
- Does it have room to breathe?
- Is it alone or next to someone?
- If it could move, where would it go?

Symbolic Expansion:

You can ask the person drawing to add details around the figure, such as a plant, an object, or another figure.

Every addition can serve as a gateway to deeper emotional exploration, opening *new avenues of inquiry* that we had not considered at all.

In a family context, you can also ask the parent to draw a figure in the place on the page where they feel safe, and open a conversation about the differences and similarities.

This is an exercise that does not *interpret* but enables. The emphasis is on presence, listening, and reaching the child as the keeper of their own secret world. The goal is to accompany them inward, with empathic curiosity.

Relationship Between Body Parts

The size of the head relative to the body, the accentuation of body parts (eyes, mouth, legs) or their absence, conveys signs that reflect the child's feelings. Do they feel strong, vulnerable, or emotionally overwhelmed?

Age and Developmental Influences

One must take the child's developmental stage into account.

For example, a 4-year-old may draw a "head with legs" figure regardless of emotional state. An 8-year-old who draws a similar figure may be expressing emotional difficulty or regression.

Proportions, Movement, and Details: The Connection to Self-Image

Comparison between drawings at different ages

This table summarizes body parts and features, and their possible interpretations in the analysis of drawings by children and adolescents from both positive and negative aspects. Naturally, everything must be understood within the context of the drawing, the person who drew it, and the various events in their life.

TABLE 8: BODY PARTS POSSIBLE INTERPRETATION, POSITIVE AND NEGATIVE

Figure Part	Possible Positive Meaning	Possible Negative Meaning
Head	Thinking, awareness, clear identity	Mental overload, emotional detachment, or a head detached from the body
Eyes	Curiosity, openness, connection with the world	Anxiety from external gaze, feeling of being monitored or exposed
Ears	Listening, sensitivity to the environment	Oversensitivity to criticism, difficulty filtering emotional information

Figure Part	Possible Positive Meaning	Possible Negative Meaning
Mouth	Emotional expression, communication, vitality	Fear of speaking, a secret, emotional suppression, or self-erasure
Teeth	Strength, vitality	Aggression, need for defense
Hair	Aesthetics, self-expression, identity	Need for control, anxiety, distorted self-image
Neck	Connection between head and body, flexibility	Disconnection between emotion and thought, feeling of strangulation
Heart/Internal Organ	Emotion, internal connection, sincerity	Overexposure, need for protection, focal trauma
Hands	Creation, connection, ability to act	Difficulty with touch, feeling of weakness or threat
Fingers	Delicacy, precision, intention	Anxiety about touch, need for control, nervousness
Nails	Boundaries, quiet strength	Covert aggression, strong defensiveness

Figure Part	Possible Positive Meaning	Possible Negative Meaning
Long Hand	Initiative, desire to reach out, openness	Emotional intrusion, need for control or boundary detachment (significant in sexual violence when combined with a short hand)
Short Hand	Caution, healthy boundaries	Difficulty connecting, feeling of blockage
Legs	Movement, stability, independence	Feeling stuck, insecurity, or difficulty moving forward
Shading on Parts	Emotional processing, inner depth	Pain, concealment, internal conflict, or threat
Unusual Additions (e.g., wings, tail, horns)	Imagination, need for freedom, unique identity	Compensation, anxiety, feeling of alienation, or need for heightened defense

Figure Part	Possible Positive Meaning	Possible Negative Meaning
Extremely Large/Small Body	Need for visibility or emotional restraint	Flooding, damaged self-image, or feeling erasure

It is also important to remember that children's drawing abilities differ by age, and this factor must be taken into account. Here is a reminder of age groups and the corresponding drawing stage:

- Ages 3-4: The figure is a circle with lines for legs/hands (a tadpole figure).
- Ages 5-6: Clear addition of limbs, face, and clothing.
- Ages 7-9: More accurate relationship between body parts, facial expressions.
- Ages 10 and up: Attempts at realism, movement, and preoccupation with identity.

But do not be confused: a 9-year-old who drew a figure like that of a 4-year-old is not necessarily developmentally delayed. They may be drawing this way due to *a particular emotional state* or due to inhibitions in the realm of self-expression.

The Figure as a Window into Interpersonal and Embodied Understanding

The figure in the drawing is not just a body, but the child's self-perception of themselves, conveyed through the figure's structure.

We can learn about:

- **Connection to the body**: Are there proportions? Are parts hidden or emphasized?
- **Sense of control**: Is the figure standing stable? Are the hands pulled to the side, forward, or clutching something?
- **Relationships with others**: Are there additional figures? Are they close or distant? Is there a connection between them? Is there eye contact between them, clasped hands, or isolation?

SUGGESTED QUESTIONS FOLLOWING A FIGURE DRAWING

GENERAL QUESTIONS ABOUT THE FIGURE

- What is the name of the figure you drew?
- How old do you think they are?
- What are they feeling right now?
- Where are they? (at home, outside, alone, with others)
- What do they most like to do?

QUESTIONS ABOUT PARTS OF THE FIGURE

- What do they see through their eyes?
- What do they want to say through their mouth?
- Why do their hands look like that?
- If their legs could walk, where would they go?
- Is there something they are hiding or keeping to themselves?

QUESTIONS ABOUT THE FIGURE'S PLACEMENT AND SPACE

- Why did you choose to place them there on the page?
- Do they have enough room to breathe?
- Are they close to or far from something important to them?
- If they could move, where would they go?

QUESTIONS ABOUT SHADING, COLORS, AND ADDITIONS

- Why did you choose to color this part?
- There are parts you left uncolored, what does that mean?
- Is there something you would like to add to the figure?

- If they could change something about themselves, what would it be?

QUESTIONS ABOUT RELATIONSHIPS AND FAMILY

- Are they alone or with someone?
- Do they have friends? Family? Someone who listens to them?
- What do they feel when someone approaches them?
- If there were another figure, how would they behave toward one another?

QUESTIONS FOR THE PARENT / THERAPIST IN RESPONSE TO THE DRAWING

- What do you feel when you see this figure?
- Do you recognize something that reminds you of the child?
- What feelings arise in you when you look at the drawing?
- What would you like to ask the child through this figure?

DRAWING EXERCISE – THE BOY WITH THE BIG NOSE

In this chapter, we discussed the topic of the figure, and I noted the sense of smell as a factor that alters a child's behavior. I mentioned an imbalance in the sensory system as an element that can even lead a child to situations of physical violence.

Let's explore a drawing that will help us understand the concept.

The Drawing

In the drawing, we see a boy in the foreground and two children standing quite a distance away from him; the three are standing with their hands behind their backs. All three appear to be smiling. Prominent elements in the drawing:

- The physical distance
- The three children are barefoot
- Their noses are relatively large and reddish
- The boy at the front with his back turned to the other children
- A backward glance toward his friends
- The pupils of the two children in the back are looking upward

Background

This drawing reached me from worried parents whose son does not like to go to kindergarten. That said, there are days when the child does go to kindergarten, but at a certain point during the day, the kindergarten teachers call the parents and report that the child has changed his behavior. After being calm during the day, around lunchtime, he becomes restless and even escalates to violent behavior.

The parents were referred to the kindergarten counselor and psychologist to check what the child's change in behavior meant.

When the parents approached me, I tried to find out with them whether something specific occurred in the kindergarten shortly before the change began.

With the parents' permission, in collaboration with the kindergarten psychologist, I conducted a behavioral observation of the children. So that my presence would not affect the children and the flow of activity, we split the observation over several days and focused on the midday hours, the hours when the child began to change his behavior.

It turned out that every day at lunchtime, two additional children joined the afternoon program run in the kindergarten. During the first three days, nothing happened. The child behaved as usual.

On the fourth day, it happened.

The children entered the kindergarten, and then the boy began to behave differently. Gradually, his behavior became restless, and at its peak, the boy pushed one of the children.

In my observation as well, we were unable to identify a factor that could change his behavior.

I asked the parents to initiate a joint drawing session with the child, with kindergarten as the central theme.

One of the drawings was the following:

We can clearly see the principle of a *linking color*, in which elements in the drawing are colored the same, hinting at and highlighting the connection between them. The red color of the nose connects to the red color of the shirt of the child in the group on the left. But what is the connection between them? Could it be that the children are treating the child with the red nose as a clown? But notice that the hands of the child with the red shirt are crossed in front, in a blocking or protective movement.

When I noticed the drawing during the session, I showed it to the parents, and we began a conversation about the drawing.

The Question Stage

I asked the child: "Is your nose red?

Why is the nose red? Did you play dress-up?"

Then the child surprised us with the answer: "No, *my nose hurts*."

"Did you get hit on the nose in kindergarten?" "*No*."

"So why does your nose hurt?" "*Because of Beni's shirt*."

"What about Beni's shirt?" "*It has a bad smell*."

It seems this conversation clarified and signaled the reason for the change in the child's behavior.

Conclusions and Addressing the Problem

In the assessment, we conducted an *olfactory sensitivity test*, and we succeeded in identifying two smells to which the child is highly sensitive. The kindergarten teachers continued the observation; now it was clear which of the two children was the trigger for the child's behavior, so tracking became easier.

One day, it happened again: the child began to change his behavior when Beni entered the kindergarten. This was not an emotional reaction against the child; it was an emotional reaction to the smell.

In a conversation with Beni's parents, and with their consent, it was decided that Beni would have extra shirts in the kindergarten for changing. Sometimes, parents do not agree to cooperate; fortunately, Beni's parents understood the situation and were glad to help.

And so it was: when Beni would enter the kindergarten, and the child began to change his behavior, the kindergarten teacher simply changed Beni's shirt. In effect, that solved the entire problem.

One drawing, one sense of smell, and one child who loses control because of it.

SEVEN

THE FAMILY DRAWING: CLOSENESS, DISTANCE, AND HIDDEN DIALOGUES

Analyzing family relationships through drawing

"The family is the first test of freedom, because it is the only thing that the free person creates by himself and for himself."

GILBERT K. CHESTERTON

THE FAMILY AS A SOURCE OF INFORMATION

In my opinion and experience, difficulties and challenges, social skills, and cognitive development, as they are expressed in drawings, are the result of the integration of the child or adolescent with their family and with their surroundings.

There are families with biological parenthood, families with adoptive parenthood, and families with same-sex parents.

The same assessment and research parameters applied to a family can also be applied within a group relationship framework. These include groups of various kinds, women's or men's groups, a football team, a youth-movement group, and even a workplace team. In each of these groups, patterns similar to those in a family are present: power struggles, ego, hierarchy, and dynamics of belonging and control. The group, like the family, constitutes an emotional and social space in which personal and interpersonal processes are expressed, and at times even reflects the family relationships of its members.

As drawing interpreters, we may receive a family drawing from a worried parent or a social worker. We can also request a spontaneous drawing of a family as part of a drawing-interpretation process conducted with a child, an adolescent, or the entire family.

ORDER, CLOSENESS, AND DISTANCE - WHAT DO THEY SAY ABOUT RELATIONSHIPS?

When a child is asked to draw their family, they usually do not reproduce the family structure as it is supposed to be, chronologically, but place each figure according to the feelings they have toward that person: warmth, love, admiration, fear, alienation, or identification.

When presented with a family drawing for assessment, we examine it from several angles. In fact, we have the option, if we choose, to obtain a unique point of view and perception from each family member. This is a significant advantage, because it enables us to understand how each of them experiences the very same event through their own eyes. To make the assessment more precise, we ask the person who drew it to answer several guiding questions that will help us decipher the symbolic, emotional, and cognitive meanings embedded in the drawing.

KEY QUESTIONS FOR OBSERVATION:

- Who was drawn first?
- Who is larger or smaller than the rest?
- Who is close to whom?
- Is there eye contact between the figures?
- Is someone at the edge of the page, or outside it?
- Is there an added figure to the family unit? Why?
- Is a figure missing from the family unit? Why?
- Let's look at the drawing and check whether the family is drawn on different levels, who is on the upper level, and who is on the lower level?

FAMILY DYNAMICS AS REFLECTED IN THE DRAWING

- A parent who is not drawn – may indicate emotional disconnection, physical absence, or a repressed feeling.
- A child drawn especially close to one of the parents – parental alliance / co-dependency.
- Figures with their backs to each other – indicates tension, anger, disconnection, or poor communication.
- A child who draws themselves outside or to the side – expresses a sense of not belonging or of being invisible.

ABSENCE OR PRESENCE OF DETAILS - THEIR MEANING

- Expressionless faces – an attempt to hide feelings, difficulty expressing emotions.
- Figures without hands or legs – a sense of helplessness or functional limitation in the family, possibly also a physical disability in the family.
- Different clothing or different drawing styles between the figures – suggests communication gaps, a sense of estrangement, differing meanings in how the figure is perceived.
- Recurrent elements (a heart, tears, weapons, a blazing sun) – may point to repressed content or anxiety.

SAMPLE DRAWING NO. 13

All the figures were drawn without mouths and eyes.

Despite the close appearance that includes holding hands, later a family secret was discovered that the child felt "must not be seen or spoken about."

AN OPEN DIALOGUE AROUND THE FAMILY DRAWING

The family drawing serves as a gateway to a sensitive yet non-intrusive conversation.

To respect the child's dignity, it is helpful to ask:

- Which figure is having the most fun?
- Who helps the most at home?
- Would you like to change anything in the drawing?
- Where do you feel safest?

TABLE 9: SIGNS AND POSSIBLE INTERPRETATION IN THE FAMILY DRAWING

Sign in the Family Drawing	Emotional Interpretation	Physical Interpretati on	Social Interpretation
Adult figure drawn very small/ in a corner	Vulnerability of the parent, fear of a specific parent	—	Weakened parenting, difficulty in the relationship
Figures without expression/ mouth/ hands	Difficulty communicating feeling of lack of control	—	Non-speaking' figures, family silence

Sign in the Family Drawing	Emotional Interpretation	Physical Interpretation	Social Interpretation
Drawing a fence/wall/ boundaries	Need to protect oneself, fear	—	Distance from the family, experience of blockage or danger
Animals/objects between family members	Emotional separation/ blockage	—	Emotional/social barrier between family members
Striking difference between the parents' drawings	Dichotomous perception between the figures	—	Identification of couple conflict, identification with one side
A figure that stands out/is alone in a different color	Feeling of being different in the family, loneliness	—	The child feels different or observed
Dark colors around the family/figure	Sadness, worry, negative experiences	—	Conflict, distance, presence of distress

Sign in the Family Drawing	Emotional Interpretation	Physical Interpretation	Social Interpretation
A figure that is not drawn (missing)	Need to hide a figure, repression	—	Repression, disconnection from family ties
Large/small figures	Dominance, apprehension, or lack of self-worth	—	Power relations, family hierarchy, fear/clinging
Strong lines around a specific figure	Strong feelings toward a figure (fear, anger, love)	—	An emotionally/ socially central figure
Vivid colors around a figure/family	Emotional energy, tension, enthusiasm	—	Strong involvement or possible conflict
The child's position in the drawing	How the child perceives their place in the family	—	Inclusion/ exclusion, sense of belonging

Sign in the Family Drawing	Emotional Interpretation	Physical Interpretati on	Social Interpretation
Figures hugging/ having physical contact	Family closeness, emotional proximity	—	Strong bonds between family members
A figure drawn far away/ separated	Emotional alienation, distance	—	Experience of loneliness in the family, conflict

FAMILY STRUCTURE IN CHILDREN'S DRAWINGS

One of the significant aspects in interpreting children's and adolescents' drawings is the family structure on the drawing page.

If the family is drawn in a single line, in a schematic structure (Father, Mother, and the children in chronological order), it has one meaning.

If the family is drawn in levels, this is a depiction of ranks or status; it matters who is on each level, and how close the person drawing feels to each figure, emotionally and physically.

In a three-tier structure, the middle level is the most significant. It represents the emotional and social core of the person drawing, the focus of attention, and those who occupy a central place in their life. The top level reflects figures perceived as more distant, sometimes physically, and sometimes emotionally. By contrast, the bottom level may indicate those whose status is lower in the drafter's eyes, and at times, even a sense of humiliation or rejection.

The placement of figures in the drawing is not accidental; it expresses the child's or adolescent's subjective perception of their relationships.

Through the family drawing, one can learn much about family dynamics: about the relationship between the parents, the internal hierarchy, overt or covert tensions, and even expressions of violence. Alongside this, the drawing may also reflect feelings of closeness, warmth, and love.

CASE STUDY – THE BOY FROM THE NORTH

Several years ago, a single mother of two children from the north approached me. In the family drawing, the boy drew himself and his mother in one row; he drew his sister in a row above them, far behind. After interpreting the drawings, I met with the mother for parental guidance sessions over three consecutive months.

At the end of this period, the boy drew the family again. Everyone was in one row, the mother on the right side, and the two siblings holding hands, with the person drawing positioned between the mother and the sibling; he is the one holding the mother's hands. This is a profound and highly significant change within three months of work. The case was very complex, involving a family with many emotional difficulties. The results, clearly seen in the drawing, made this one of the cases that moved me most over my twenty years of work.

THE MEANING OF THE SUN IN DRAWINGS BY CHILDREN, ADOLESCENTS, AND ADULTS.

The sun is a recurring element in family drawings. One out of three drawings includes the sun (33%). Sometimes it is drawn large, at the top left, and sometimes as a warm circle in the center of the page, as well as in many other places across the drawing page.

Studies focusing on *children's drawings* show that the sun is a *symbol of the bond between the person drawing and the mother*, the source of warmth, life, and light how the child interprets the mother's attitude toward them.

How do they understand the mother's relationship with them and with the family as a whole?

On the other hand, in studies that focus on *relationships*, researchers have not succeeded in finding a connection between the sun and the relationship between mother and child.

Position of the Sun on the Right Side Position of the sun on the right side of the page is not accidental; it carries deep symbolic meaning. In the chapter dealing with the division of the drawing page, we learned that the right side represents the social and extra-familial world: work, studies, and relationships outside the family. When the sun is located on this side, it may hint at a feeling of lack or absence of the mother, whether due to her external occupations or due to emotional detachment. In some cases, such a placement may indicate a real absence of the mother, such as death, prolonged illness, or divorce. The sun, as a symbol of warmth, presence, and enlightenment, may reflect the mother's place in the child's life, and sometimes her absence.

Position of the Sun on the Left Side

Positioning the sun on the left side of the page carries deep symbolic meaning. The left side in the drawing is perceived as an internal, emotional, familial, embracing space, and therefore a sun placed there may hint at a mother perceived as home-oriented, present, connected to the family, and to her parental role. However, to understand whether she is also perceived as a good mother, we must examine the other signs in the drawing.

A Large, Shining Sun

A large, shining sun that stands out in its color and placement may reflect a sense of security, emotional warmth, and positive maternal presence. By contrast, a dim sun, floating far away, or not drawn at all, can indicate an experience of emotional deprivation, distancing, or detachment from the mother, whether physical or emotional.

A red sun with caressing rays – sometimes points to an ambivalent (two-sided) relationship with the mother, love and pain together.

The Significance of the Length of the Sun's Rays –

The length of the sun's rays indicates how close and embracing the mother's manner of relating is. At times, one can also see the direction of the rays, which are focused on one child in the family more than on another.

Sometimes it is possible to notice a change in the length of the ray (long or short), which indicates instability or lack of continuity in the relationship as experienced by the child who is drawing.

Significance of the Shape of the Sun's Rays

The shape of the rays reflects the mother's warmth, love, criticalness, aggression, or softness, all according to the child's perception.

Significance of the Density of the Sun's Rays

One can learn about frequency, whether the mother is *intrusive* or allows breathing room and development, and a personal space.

Example Drawing No. 14 - A black sun with sharp rays

It turned out that the relationship with the mother is accompanied by fears and a constant sense of criticism directed toward the child.

TOOLS FOR CREATING CHANGE THROUGH THE FAMILY DRAWING

For the work with the family, with the assistance of the drawing analysis, I developed three therapeutic models that we will discuss in the chapter on treatment models: the models are "Family Sits to Draw," "Projection: From Childhood to Parenthood," and "The Collaborative Drawing."

Here are a few things one can do...

- To draw the family as he/she would like it to be, and discuss the differences.
- Suggest drawing of the family as animals, and ask why each animal was chosen.
- Suggest drawing the same drawing in the future – at age 20 or 30.
- To jointly create an imaginary family page – to allow healing through projection.

Professional recommendation:

The family drawing is an intimate and profound window, but also very sensitive.

We must maintain empathy and caution in interpretation; our role is to *listen.*

EIGHT

MOVEMENT, LINE, AND BODY, MOTOR SKILLS, AND THEIR IMPACT ON DRAWING

The connection between physical skill and graphic emotional expression

"The line the child's hand draws is not only a bodily movement; it is evidence of a feeling that found a way to pass through the body to the paper."

ASSESSING FINE AND GROSS MOTOR SKILLS THROUGH DRAWING

Not every difficulty in drawing stems from emotional distress. Sometimes, broken lines, crooked shapes, or a lack of proportion simply derive from a motor difficulty that is not always diagnosed.

- Fine motor skills – pencil grip, ability to control lines, accuracy in details.
- Gross motor skills – overall posture, eye–hand coordination, control of the body during drawing.

Difficulties in coordinating fine and gross motor skills are expressed in a drawing that is *messy, with lines that stray beyond the boundaries, and inconsistent pressure.*

EXAMPLES

CASE 1: DIFFICULTY CLOSING THE CIRCLE IN THE HEAD OUTLINE

A 6-year-old girl draws figures but struggles to close the circle of the head outline.

The girl experiences a lack of confidence around graphic tasks. This affects her socially, both in the classroom due to the many graphic tasks, and in social encounters after school.

Recommended Intervention:

- Practice through play: use worksheets with cute figures that "need a head", the girl will be asked to complete the circle. This can be turned into a game where every circle she closes "saves" the figure.
- Use of aids: Suggest using circle templates (like a bottle cap) to feel immediate success, and then gradually move to freehand drawing.
- Positive reinforcement: Every time she manages to close a circle, even if it's not perfect, it's important *to praise her for persistence, not only for the result.*

CASE 2: DIFFICULTY COPYING GEOMETRIC SHAPES

A 6-year-old girl struggles to copy simple shapes like a square or triangle from the board to her notebook. She tends to give up midway or erase repeatedly, which leaves her feeling frustrated and incapable. In class, she avoids taking part in activities that require drawing or copying, and sometimes even asks to leave the lesson. Her classmates notice her difficulty and sometimes offer help in ways that embarrass her. Even outside school hours, she avoids games that involve crafts or drawing, which reduces her opportunities to integrate socially.

Recommended intervention:

- Use three-dimensional materials: Work with blocks, plastic, or cardboard triangles, first through touch, then drawing. This increases spatial understanding and reduces pressure.
- Turn the task into a story: The triangle is a superhero's tent; let's draw it so they can go inside. *Bringing imagination into it reduces anxiety and boosts motivation.*
- Work in pairs: Practice with a supportive classmate to turn the task into a positive social experience.

CASE 3: DIFFICULTY FILLING AREAS AND CHOOSING COLORS

A boy struggles to choose colors and to fill areas evenly. He tends to go out of the lines, which leads him to feel that his drawing is *not pretty or not like the others*'. He compares himself to his peers and feels inferior, leading to the avoidance of creative tasks. In class, he sometimes turns in a blank page or one with a partial drawing. In social gatherings, when the children draw together, he sits on the side or asks to do something else, which leads to social distancing and a sense of loneliness.

Recommended intervention:

- Use thick crayons or thin markers: Teach coloring in stages, first the interior of the shape; then, with thin markers, color the areas close to the lines. This allows faster, more precise filling and reduces frustration.
- Guidance through open questions: Instead of saying "color nicely", ask him, "Which color do you think suits the character's dress?" This encourages personal expression.
- Create a small art exhibition: Displaying his drawings in class or at home strengthens a sense of pride and belonging.

HOW DO WE ADDRESS THESE DIFFICULTIES?

Exemplary Plan for Drawing and Emotional Reinforcement for a 6-Year-Old Girl

STAGE 1: CREATING EXPERIENCES OF SUCCESS IN DRAWING

Goal: to reduce anxiety and strengthen a sense of competence

Tailored tasks: worksheets with guiding lines, circle templates, and pre-drawn shapes to complete.

Supporting tools: thick markers, gouache paints, stickers – anything that produces an impressive result even with minimal effort.

Joint drawing: you draw one part, and she completes it – this creates a sense of partnership and reduces pressure.

STAGE 2: INTEGRATING DRAWING INTO SOCIAL PLAY

Goal: to turn drawing into a social tool rather than a source of frustration

Role-play with drawing: for example, "Draw me a treasure map", or "Let's draw the fairies' city together".

Group creation: working on a shared poster with other children – each contributes a small part.

Using favorite characters: drawing characters from movies or books she loves to boost motivation.

STAGE 3: EMOTIONAL REINFORCEMENT THROUGH DIALOGUE

Goal: to process feelings around difficulty and empower the girl

Simple emotional dialogue: How did you feel when you closed the circle? Or what did you like most about your drawing?

Drawing journal: a notebook in which she draws something small every day, and you write an encouraging sentence for her.

Mirroring successes: show her progress over time – "Look how you've improved since the first drawing!"

DISTINGUISHING BETWEEN A TECHNICAL ISSUE AND AN EMOTIONAL ONE

It is important not to rush to interpret a vague or "messy" drawing as a sign of distress; it may be a purely motor difficulty.

However, sometimes the drawing difficulty itself becomes part of the child's emotional experience.

THE MEANING OF LINE TYPES AND HAND MOVEMENTS

The line in a drawing is a messenger – it conveys power, helplessness, control, or turmoil:

- Strong, pressed, very dark lines usually indicate internal tension, a need for control, or inner turmoil.
- Weak, faded, broken lines – may point to fatigue, avoidance, over-caution, or emotional difficulty.
- Very rapid or messy lines – dysregulation, haste, impulsivity, or difficulty with organization.

- Repetitive lines (layers, erasures, reinforcements) – sometimes related to difficulties with emotional regulation or obsessive thinking; a need to hide something. Sometimes the erasing is done to show that something is wrong, and the erasure prompts the therapist to ask questions about it, thereby exposing what was erased.

TOOLS FOR CREATING CHANGE THROUGH EXPLORING THE LINE AND MOTOR ACTIVITY

- Ask the child to draw with pencils of different thicknesses and examine the sense of control.
- Use markers, watercolors, or chalk to diversify the sensory experience and willingness to experiment.
- Integrate physical movement before drawing to support regulation and gross motor skills.
- Offer free drawing accompanied by music, focusing on rhythm, release, and emotional expression.
- Ask the child to choose two colors that feel safe and draw free lines with them.

Professional note: It is important to be attentive to see when the technical difficulty becomes an emotional message.

The goal is not to improve drawing skills, but to restore to the child the experience of control, being seen, and expression, even with a trembling finger.

NINE

FRIENDSHIPS AND LEARNING DIFFICULTIES

Identifying social skills and learning skills through drawing

"A child's drawing not only expresses their world, but it also reflects their social skills and learning skills."

IDENTIFYING LEARNING SKILLS THROUGH DRAWING

Through the drawing, we can learn about the abilities and skills of the person who drew it. Early identification of difficulty or slowness on the developmental path enables us to provide tools earlier that may be life-changing.

In the previous chapter, we discussed identifying motor abilities and motor development; in this chapter, we will learn about learning skills and social skills.

In the following tables: Identifying Learning Skills and Social Skills Through Drawing, you will find examples of features in the domain of learning skills as they appear in drawings, and what each feature may mean.

TABLE 10: IDENTIFYING LEARNING SKILLS THROUGH DRAWING

Feature in Drawing	Possible Meaning	Concrete Example
Order and Organization in Space	Ability to plan, organize information, cognitive regulation	The child draws a tidy study desk with book, writing tools, and without clutter.
Use of Small Details	Concentration, precision, ability to distinguish details.	The child adds blinds to the classroom window, books on a shelf, figures with names.
Transition Between Parts of the Drawing	Mental flexibility, understand sequence, planning	The girl draws a story in stages: a figure waking up, going to school, participating in a lesson.
Use of Varied Colors	Creativity, emotional expression, symbolic understanding.	A different color for each figure according to feeling: blue for calm, red for enthusiasm and assertiveness.

Feature in Drawing	Possible Meaning	Concrete Example
Drawing of a Learning Scene (Classroom, Books)	Positive connection to learning, sense of belonging to the framework.	The girl draws herself in the classroom, pointing to an answer, smiling, a teach talking to her.

TABLE 11: SOCIAL SKILLS THROUGH DRAWING.

Social Element in Drawing	Social Skills	Concrete Example
Figures in Interaction	Communication, Cooperation	The child draws two figures playing with a ball, with positive facial expressions and physical closeness between them.
Distance Between Figures	Boundaries, Intimacy	The girl draws herself in one corner, with classmates far away, conveying a feeling of loneliness or a need for privacy.

Social Element in Drawing	**Social Skills**	**Concrete Example**
Clear Facial Expressions	Empathy, Emotional Reading	The figures in the drawing are smiling or sad, making it possible to identify emotions and understand the social situation.
Body Language	Non-Verbal Understanding	The child draws a figure touching another figure on the back, expressing support or friendship.
Social Situation	Group Functioning	The girl draws a school lunch scene, with figures around a table, conversing, and showing physical closeness.
Placement of Figures in Space	Sense of Belonging	The child draws himself in the center of a group of friends, all smiling, with an open circle of friends around him.

WHAT ARE WE ACTUALLY LOOKING FOR?

We are looking for signs of confidence, belonging, or social anxiety in the child's drawings. Does the child reveal their standing within a group? Do they feel wanted, present, and that they belong?

- Many figures, close together and smiling - a sense of belonging and security in the social space.
- Figures with their backs to each other or without eyes - communication difficulties, emotional distance.
- Isolated self or drawn far from the others - an experience of loneliness, social anxiety, or rejection.
- Avoiding drawing people altogether - sometimes hints at profound social difficulty or trauma.
- The child drew an entire class and set themselves outside the group.

THE CONNECTION BETWEEN LEARNING MOTIVATION AND THE DRAWING CONTENT

A drawing can offer a clue to the child's educational experience: how the child experiences success and difficulty, and how the system supports or challenges them.

- *An orderly and clear drawing, with many details,* may indicate motivation, effort, and

identification with the educational environment.

- *An empty, scribbled, or unfinished drawing* - sometimes reflects an experience of failure, worthlessness, or difficulty with attention and concentration.
- *Drawings with educational symbols (books, a teacher, a classroom)* - enable a discussion of feelings toward school.
- *A supportive and containing environment* usually allows for free, creative, and detailed drawings.
- *A demanding, judgmental, or competitive environment* can lead to avoidance, frequent erasures, and fear of mistakes.

TOOLS FOR CREATING CHANGE THROUGH SOCIO-EDUCATIONAL DRAWING

- Draw one good thing that happened to me today – and ask why.
- Invite the child to draw friends according to who is closest to them – and then draw friends again according to who they would like to be close to them.

- Encourage the child to draw the school as an imaginary place – what would they want the school to look like?
- Draw my success – and then write what helped me succeed.

When children struggle with words, it is sometimes easier for them to draw what they feel in the classroom or among friends. It is important not only to see what they draw, but also to understand what they do not draw, and how they talk about it.

TEN

THE ANIMALS THAT SPEAK EMOTIONS: AN EMOTIONAL LEXICON FOR ANIMALS IN DRAWINGS

Interpretation of animals, insects, and reptiles on the drawn page

---

> "**An animal does not ask about your past and does not judge your future; it responds only to your essence now, and thus reminds a person to be truly present.**"

THE PERSON, THE ANIMAL, AND THE RELATIONSHIP BETWEEN THEM

In quite a few children's and adolescents' drawings, animals appear. They are part of the day-to-day reality, and *they carry emotional, cultural, and symbolic meaning*. Every animal can be *part of a positive message or part of a negative message*. We may encounter drawings in which the same animal is drawn twice in the same drawing, but with a different message.

The animal can serve as:

- An emotional symbol: power, fear, comfort, self-worth.
- An agent of family dialogue: Who is represented by the animal? To whom does it belong? What is the reaction to it?
- An internal projection: The animal as self-representation or a significant figure.
- A connecting thread between worlds: reality, imagination, dream, and memory

For children, animals embody forces and feelings that are hard for them to contain or express themselves, whether it is power, aggression, vulnerability, protection, or a longing for warmth, love, relationships, and intimacy.

In this chapter, we will learn about the traits and signs that the animal brings, as a positive message or as a negative message. Try to connect with the animal you love most, an animal that represents you.

TABLE 12: COMMON ANIMALS IN DRAWINGS - POSITIVE AND NEGATIVE EMOTIONAL MESSAGE

Animal	Common Positive Message	Possible Negative Message
Dog	Loyalty, Protection, Friendship	Dependency, Excessive devotion
Cat	Independence, Sensitivity	Emotional detachment, Suspicion
Horse	Freedom, Inner strength	Need to escape, Difficulty committing
Turtle/ Tortoise	Patience, Self-protection	Withdrawal, Stagnation/Freezing
Bear	Gentle strength, Family warmth	Unconscious aggression
Snake	Transformation, Deep wisdom	Threat, Cunning, Sexual anxiety
Bird	Longing for the spirit, Emotional freedom	Escape from reality, Disconnection from the ground
Lion	Inner authority, Self-confidence	Dominance, Need for control
Wolf	Leadership, Connection to the pack	Loneliness, Environment threat

Animal	Common Positive Message	Possible Negative Message
Butterfly	Gentle change, Emotional healing	Temporariness, Fear of impermanence
Mouse	Sensitivity, discernment	Cowardice, Helplessness
Bee	Hard work, Order	Overload, Imbalance
Owl	Intuition, Inner wisdom	Disconnection, Observing from the side
Rabbit	Innocence, Speed of reaction	Anxiety, Instability
Monkey	Playfulness, Social interaction	Recklessness, Need for distractions
Crocodile	Hidden power, Deep protection	Covert danger, Aggression from repression
Cow	Nurturing, Inner calm	Conventionality/Monotony, Lack of boundaries
Giraffe	Perspective, Heightened gentleness	Disconnection from reality, Fantasy
Beetle	Resilience, Modesty	Over-transparency, Lack of presence

Animal	Common Positive Message	Possible Negative Message
Spider	Creativity, Connectivity	Manipulation, Fear of temptation

Each animal conveys, in its own way, the message the person drawing wants to communicate, using the animal's traits, its appearance, and the character qualities they connect with to represent them and the feeling they are experiencing at the time of the drawing.

Here are several examples of cards you can create yourself. On each card: the animal's name, its appearance, how it appears in the drawing, the positive or negative message, and a question for the facilitator, parent, or therapist.

Here are several exemplary entries:

Name: Owl

Typical appearance: Large eyes, calm gaze, symmetrical body.

In the drawing: Often appears alone, watching from the side, or at the center of the drawing like a "keeper of secrets."

Positive emotional message: Inner wisdom, deep perception, quiet presence.

Negative emotional message: Emotional detachment, observation without involvement, a sense of "I don't belong."

Question for the parent/therapist: What does the child think the owl knows? Does the child allow the owl to know things about them?

Name: Wolf

Typical appearance: Thick fur, sharp eyes, sometimes a frontal gaze.

In the drawing: Alone in a snowy landscape or part of a group in the background; sometimes hovering between contact and distance with the children.

Positive emotional message: Loyalty to the pack, group intuition, strength in listening.

Negative emotional message: A feeling of loneliness, threat, or a hidden presence of fear.

Question for the parent/therapist: Does the child feel part of any pack? Does the wolf represent someone close or the child themself?

Name: Butterfly

Typical appearance: Colorful wings, small body, light movement.

In the drawing: Above a figure, near a flower, sometimes alone against an empty background.

Positive emotional message: A process of change, inner softness, connection to the world of emotion.

Negative emotional message: Fear of impermanence, a feeling of fragility in the face of the world.

Question for the parent/therapist: At what point of change is the child? Is there fear or hope in the wings?

Name: Snake

Typical appearance: Flexible body, piercing eyes, spiral or segmented movement.

In the drawing: Underground, coiling around an object or figure.

Positive emotional message: Ability to renew, intuitive wisdom, unstable boundaries.

Negative emotional message: Threat, cunning, conflict around sexuality or secrecy.

Question for the parent/therapist: Is there something the child keeps deep inside? Is the snake frightening or protective?

Name: Elephant

Typical appearance: A massive body, kind eyes, a long trunk.

In the drawing: Present as a "big father," sometimes beside a small child or a tree.

Positive emotional message: Stability, deep emotional memory, protective presence.

Negative emotional message: Excessive responsibility, internal heaviness, difficulty with emotional expression.

Question for the parent/therapist: Does the child feel "too big" for their place in the family or in society?

Name: Bee

Typical appearance: A small body with stripes, swift wings, vibrating movement.

In the drawing: Next to a flower, in a group, or in conflictual areas of the drawing.

Positive emotional message: Devotion, order, group functioning.

Negative emotional message: Emotional overload, need to impress, silent exhaustion.

Question for the parent/therapist: Is the child busy "performing," or wishing to be loved unconditionally?

Name: Lion

Typical appearance: A large mane, a strong gaze, golden-brown hues.

In the drawing: A central presence, sometimes solitary or with a distant, heavenward gaze.

Positive emotional message: Inner authority, self-confidence, self-respect.

Negative emotional message: Domineering, need for external proof, seeking approval through power.

Question for the parent/therapist: Who is the "king" in the child's life? Does the child experience it as a burden or as protection?

Name: Zebra

Typical appearance: Black-and-white stripes, a delicate yet distinct body.

In the drawing: At the margins of the drawing or in a group, sometimes near human figures.

Positive emotional message: Integration of opposites, uniqueness, ability to blend in.

Negative emotional message: Inner conflict, a feeling of fragmentation, visibility without permanence.

Question for the parent/therapist: Is the child trying to connect different worlds within? What is the black and what is the white?

Name: Fish

Typical appearance: A flowing body, often colorful or semi-transparent.

In the drawing: In water, sometimes in a closed environment such as an aquarium.

Positive emotional message: Inner flow, connection to quiet emotion, healing presence.

Negative emotional message: Sense of imprisonment, difficulty expressing emotions, excessive transparency.

Question for the parent/therapist: Does the child feel they are "swimming" alone? Does the water calm or confine?

Name: Cricket

Typical appearance: A small body, long legs, an almost invisible appearance.

In the drawing: At the margins of the drawing, sometimes as a point of sound or movement.

Positive emotional message: Listening, sensitivity to space, ability to notice details.

Negative emotional message: Sense of insignificance, fear that the voice is not heard.

Question for the parent/therapist: Does the child express themselves through hints? Is the cricket asking to be heard?

Name: Gorilla

Typical appearance: A massive body, a deep gaze, large hands.

In the drawing: Close to the central figure or as a protective parent.

Positive emotional message: Strength that contains, gentle protection, a mature presence.

Negative emotional message: Concern about aggression, fear of inner power that is not understood.

Question for the parent/therapist: Does the gorilla represent a protective or a threatening figure? Where does the child find strength?

DIALOGUES BETWEEN ANIMALS IN CHILDREN'S DRAWINGS

Just like human beings, sometimes the conversation is between two of the same type of animal, sometimes between two different animals.

The child who is drawing personifies figures in their life as animals. This is certainly an interesting area in which to examine the connection between the animal world and the child's reality.

WHAT CAN AN ANIMAL DIALOGUE IN A DRAWING REPRESENT?

- A conversation between internal parts of the child: A protective dog versus an aggressive snake: Is the child in a process of reconciliation between fear and trust?
- A reflection of family dynamics: A tall giraffe versus a small mouse: Perhaps representing an emotionally distant parent versus a child who cannot reach them.
- A struggle between feelings: A quiet owl versus a jumping monkey: Is the child deliberating between the quiet they need and the noise of the environment?
- Friendship or alienation: A running horse versus a watching cat: Perhaps the child dreams of freedom but feels disconnected.

ANIMALS IN DIALOGUE - INTERPRETATION

Animals also engage in a dialogue between themselves; each one can represent a figure in the life of the person drawing, perhaps two inner figures, dilemmas, or an inner dialogue. And of course, they can be the fruit of a rich imagination. Here are several possible examples of combining animals and the dialogue between them.

Dog versus Cat

Dog in the drawing: usually in motion, close to figures, an open presence.

Cat in the drawing: watching from the side, quiet, sometimes on a fence or at a distance.

The dialogue: the dog approaches, the cat retreats. Is the child seeking closeness that is met with suspicion? Is there a conflict between the desire for closeness and the need for boundaries?

Question for the parent/therapist: Does the child identify with one of the animals, or with the dynamic between them? Is there someone in their environment who comes across to them as a "dog" or a "cat"?

Elephant versus Butterfly

The elephant in the drawing: large, protective, a steady presence

The butterfly in the drawing: fluttering nearby, light, colorful

The dialogue: the elephant guards, the butterfly wants to move. Is the child expressing a simultaneous need for stability and freedom? Do they feel a heaviness that hinders movement?

Question for the parent/therapist: What is the relationship between weight and gentleness in the child's life? Is there someone trying to protect them and someone who is pulling them to break free?

Turtle versus Monkey

The turtle in the drawing: slow, protective, sitting quietly in a defined area

The monkey in the drawing: jumping, amusing, extremely active

The dialogue: the turtle stays inside, the monkey seeks movement. This is a struggle between withdrawal and expression, between self-protection and activity.

Question for the therapist/parent: Is the child torn between the wish "to stay with themselves" and the urge "to go out into the world"? Which do they identify with more?

Swan versus Spider

The swan in the drawing: gliding quietly, usually alone, surrounded by gentle water

The spider in the drawing: building webs, operating without a striking visual presence

The dialogue: the swan maintains harmony, the spider weaves connections. Does the child dream of calm yet feel entangled in relationships?

Question for the therapist/parent: Is the swan the fantasy, and the spider the reality? Does the child feel that their movement depends on others?

Dolphin versus Crocodile

The dolphin in the drawing: bright colors, flowing movement, an open eye

The crocodile in the drawing: half hidden in the water, mouth open, or with a concealed gaze

The dialogue: the dolphin represents communication and lightness, the crocodile represents quiet power and a hidden threat.

Question for the therapist/parent: Does the child feel they have to "walk between the raindrops", to be available yet wary of pain?

Dove versus Owl

The dove in the drawing: white, in the light, symbolizes peace and gentleness

The owl in the drawing: darker, observant, often alone

The dialogue: the dove wants to connect, the owl keeps its distance. Is this a dialogue between emotional openness and the need to remain an observer?

Question for the therapist/parent: Does the child express feelings from a place of trust, or keep them "quiet" like the owl?

Important to know: You can ask the child to draw an animal, even during a full interpretation process, as an addition to those standard drawings. You can also go further and ask for a bad animal and a good animal to open another, more focused conversation.

ELEVEN

WHEN PAIN APPEARS IN THE DRAWING

Signs of Violence and Sexual Violence

Sensitive ways to distinguish between a sign and a deep emotional break!

SOMETHING PERSONAL ON THE SUBJECT

When it comes to the field of interpreting drawings by children, adolescents, and families, I see signs of violence and sexual violence as among the most important issues, if not the most important. This is the most extreme place, the deepest abyss, to which a child, adolescent, or adult can reach. An abyss that brings them to a point where words do not come out of their mouth; they come out only through the drawing.

At the age of ten, I was sexually assaulted by an adolescent from the school I attended. An assault that shook my life.

In those days, at home, in the family, there was no one who could hear me, listen to me, or see me.

Even at school, they were not prepared to handle such an incident; they did not know how to treat me with this difficult case.

The entire incident, and the days that followed, ultimately sank into my subconscious. There was not a day I did not recall the incident; I did not deny it, I did not repress it, not for a moment. The event always remained in my day-to-day experience, to this very day. The case undoubtedly affected the entire course of my life as a child, an adolescent, a husband, and a father.

Years later, even before I began my academic studies, I was exposed to the field of interpreting children's drawings. During an in-class exercise, as we drew, everything was released from me. The incident in which I was sexually assaulted came back to me, as if it were happening at that very moment I was drawing – everything poured out onto the page. During the process, I felt my body begin to sweat and tremble, and I understood that something significant was happening.

At that moment, I had no idea, yet I understood that I had come to a field and a tool through which I could help children and adolescents who experience violence in any form. I understood that I could give them a tool to illuminate the darkness they are in. From there, I could give them tools to step out into the light. This is where my mission truly began.

Interpreting drawings by children, adolescents, and families has held a central and significant place for me throughout my entire career.

I also understood the great responsibility I carry: to act with heightened vigilance so as not to harm anyone living their life within such events.

For me, interpreting drawings by children, adolescents, and families is, in fact, a hand extended to a child, adolescent, or adult who is in a vortex, a quagmire, or a deep abyss, a hand that will bring him, her, or them back to a safe place.

DIFFERENT TYPES OF VIOLENCE

Violence is a forceful act intended to injure, harm, abuse, or destroy. It can be physical, verbal, emotional, sexual, social, or financial, as long as it carries an intent to harm or has a harmful impact on a person, a group, animals, or property.

There are quite a few types of violence in society. In recent years, as social networks have strengthened, new forms of violence have emerged. We can point specifically to *shaming violence*, in which practically anyone can harm and defame another person *with no possibility of defense,* as well as other, more severe and violent cases.

Interpreting drawings by children, adolescents, and families makes it possible to identify signs that may indicate exposure to or an experience of violence. This assists law enforcement officials, as well as social work and welfare professionals (Social Services) identifying children and adolescents at risk. The drawing carries information, signs, and certain parameters that can be learned from the following table.

TABLE 13: DIFFERENT TYPES OF VIOLENCE

Type of Violence	Possible Signs in Drawings	General Characteristics
Physical Violence	Figures with signs of injury, use of red color, drawing of weapons, sharp lines, figure missing limbs.	Physical injuries, hitting, pushing, scratching, bruises.
Verbal Violence	Speech bubbles with hard words, figures with mouths open screaming, small figures against large threatening ones	Curses, humiliation, screaming, threats.
Emotional Violence	Isolated figures, dark colors, expressionless faces, many erasures, a feeling of emptiness or suppression.	Neglect/Ignorance, consistent humiliation, invalidation of feelings, psychological control.
Sexual Violence	Drawings with emphasized body parts, intrusive lines, nude figures, a feeling of discomfort in the drawing.	Unwanted touch, sexual exploitation, exposure to sexual content.

MAIN TYPES OF VIOLENCE AS THEY APPEAR IN DRAWINGS

Physical Violence

Distorted figures, missing or emphasized body parts (hands, legs), strong and broken lines, drawings of violent scenes, bodily injuries, blood, weapons.

Sexual Violence

Absence, shading, distortion of intimate parts, mouth or chin blocked or erased, lower body disconnected or shaded, hollow eyes, suggestive scenes.

Emotional or Psychological Violence

Isolated, small, or humiliated figures; expressionless figures; recurring dark colors; absent figures, especially the figure of the *aggressor* or the *drawer*; unstable or erased lines; many erasures; figures without eyes or mouth.

Neglect

Lack of drawing details; a house without windows or doors; figures without clothes or details; a sparsely detailed environment; figures distant from each other; absence of trees, sun, friends.

Important: Do not draw definitive conclusions from a single drawing; attending to context, recurrence, and cross-referencing data with additional sources is essential for responsible interpretation.

CURRENT STATISTICS ON VIOLENCE AGAINST CHILDREN

In 2023, 216 cases were opened in Israel for offenses of adult violence against children in educational settings (13% fewer than in 2022, yet still higher than the years that preceded it).

TABLE 14: DISTRIBUTION OF TYPES OF OFFENSES IN EDUCATIONAL SETTINGS (2018-2023)

Type of Violence	Up to Age 3 (in %)	Ages 3 to 6 (in %)
Assault (including injury)	47%	62%
Physical/Psychological Abuse	30%	20%

Type of Violence	Up to Age 3 (in %)	Ages 3 to 6 (in %)
Sexual Offenses	0.5%	4%
Neglect and Negligent Supervision	9%	6%
Threats	2%	4%
Obligation to Report (Non-compliance)	11%	4%

Data from recent years show that *children under age 6* are *the most vulnerable group to violence by adults in institutional settings.*

Rise in reports:

The number of cases reported nationwide has increased by tens of percent over the past decade, mainly thanks to increased awareness.

KEY POINTS

- *Children exposed to violence* sometimes respond in drawings with avoidance, turbulent imagery, frightening scenes, or an *overrepresentation* of specific body parts.
- Interpreting drawings as a diagnostic tool must be cautious and responsible; every sign requires a thorough, sensitive inquiry, aligned with the drawer's developmental and cultural stage.
- The data and interpretations are based on professional literature, official reports, and current research in the field of interpreting children's drawings, alongside statistical data from the Police and the National Council for the Child.

DIRECT AND INDIRECT SIGNS OF VIOLENCE

There are drawings that reach the interpreter and include relatively clear signs. However, in most cases, the signs that appear in a drawing are indirect, implied, and require careful interpretation, based on thorough familiarity with the child's personal history and a comprehensive view of the broader context.

Long Arm Syndrome

Over the years of my work in interpreting drawings of violence and sexual violence through children's drawings, I coined a term I have been using for many years: "*Long Arm Syndrome*". The label is given to a recurring phenomenon with a high prevalence in drawings of violence, especially sexual violence. In such drawings, the violent *aggressor* appears with one arm of normal length relative to the body's proportions, and the other arm is very long, sometimes reaching all the way to the victim, even if the victim is drawn very far from the aggressor in the drawing.

Body Parts Under Clothing

In a number of drawings in which sexual violence is expressed, genitals, male or female, may appear exposed. However, their appearance does not necessarily indicate sexual assault. At times, it is a child who grew up in a family where nudity is not taboo, such as cases of bathing together or a relaxed attitude toward nudity at home.

Therefore, we must exercise extra caution in this area.

There is one case in which the probability of assault rises significantly: *when the organs are drawn under the clothing*. As if the child who drew it wants to say: *I am clothed, but something is happening to me under my clothes.*

So, pay special attention when the genitals are drawn under the clothes; a red flag should go up for you.

ADDITIONAL POSSIBLE SIGNS:

- Holes or tears in the page – excessive pressure, erasures, reinforcement of lines up to the point of perforation.
- Figures that are injured, cut, or missing body parts – a hint of feeling harmed, loss of control, trauma.
- Weapons, blood, and graphic violence – may indicate exposure to harmful content or violent experiences.
- Absence of body parts related to sexuality (mouth, genitals, eyes) – may suggest sexual trauma or denial.
- Tiny figures facing giant figures – indicate unbalanced power dynamics, a sense of threat or fear.

The violence is not necessarily physical or visible. Sometimes the atmosphere of the drawing conveys fear and anxiety despite physical proximity, and at times, as in the first investigation drawing we will see, the atmosphere is good and cheerful, while the violence or danger is implied.

We will now move on to the investigation of two drawings from which we can learn about possible violence...

INVESTIGATING DRAWINGS OF VIOLENCE

HAPPY BIRTHDAY...?

The Drawing

When we look at the drawing, we notice a birthday celebration for a six-year-old girl. Three girls are at the front, close to the table and the cake. Slightly behind them on the left, there is another boy; everyone is happy and cheering at the birthday party. At the top right, a figure is placed in a very prominent way. It was impossible to ignore this figure from the very first glance, but for the purpose of this explanation, I ignored the figure for a moment.

The figure in the background is an adult. The facial features look like those of a tough person, someone who has been through quite a lot, and if we generalize for a moment, he has the appearance of a violent, very strong man. What is he doing there?

Analysis of the Drawing

As I noted earlier, one possibility in a drawing is that the overall image depicts a particular situation or event, which is happy, in this case, while additional, hidden messages are conveyed in parallel that suggest otherwise.

I recommend creating a standard analysis pathway with which to investigate every drawing. Such a pathway streamlines the work and increases the accuracy of the results.

THE COLORS

The combination: cheerful colors, a bit of red, light blue, greenish, and yellow. Yellow: teaches us about warmth and love, but beyond the yellow in the flags, the overall hue of the picture is yellow. This element makes us less enthusiastic about the joy, about the birthday event. Here, yellow serves as a filter, a hint that something is not right in the event we see in the drawing.

Light blue: among other things that light blue tells us as a color, it signals a need for protection and emotional space. Light blue also tells us about a rich imagination and a tendency to escape from pressing reality.

In the drawing, we see that light blue appears on each of the children (the hats), and also on the shirt of the girl on the right.

Note: the colors of the flags are identical to the colors of the shirts of the girls at the table.

PLACEMENT OF THE FIGURES

In analyzing the placement of the figures, we will refer to each figure separately and begin to analyze the structure of the group in the drawing.

In the chapter about the group (family), we learned that when a group is drawn in two rows, one above the other, this carries meaning regarding the importance of the people in each row in the eyes of the person drawing. In the first row, close to the cake table, we can see the girls, who are close friends. They are undoubtedly the center of the drawing's story. In the top row are the adult figures on the right, and on the left, the young boy, who apparently is somewhat socially distant from the girls at the center of the table.

The adult figure at the top right essentially comes from outside the party, outside the event, and seems to be peeking into it. The feeling the figure conveys is fear, threat, and forcefulness.

SUMMARY OF THE DRAWING'S INTERPRETATION

There is a joyful event here, a birthday celebration. The participants look happy and close, even physically, side by side. The flags at the top left form the shape of a sun, with the flags as the sun's rays. The sun (mother) is present at the event, and not by chance; the girl needs the mother's presence in the environment.

Alongside the cheerful atmosphere, the drawing carries an unequivocal message of an external threat; the person on the left is the threatening figure.

We sense a violent atmosphere. The question is, who is actually the threatening figure? Perhaps it is the father? Perhaps another family member? Who is the threat directed at? Maybe all the children together? Or at one of the children in the drawing?

The shared color of the hats gives a sense of connection among the children. Are we dealing with a threat coming from the adult?

Please note: The color of the shirt of the girl on the right is the same light blue as the hats. Is there a connection?

There are also cases in a drawing where the child who draws is actually telling the story of another person who appears in the drawing. So, it is certainly possible that this is the story of the girl with the light-blue shirt.

In conclusion: From this drawing and the symbols that emerge from it, my line of thought, also because of the size and placement of the threatening figure, is that there is a real threat to all the children participating in the birthday party.

The presence of the mother (an implied sun) inside the house hints at the need for the mother's protection; she serves as a balancing counterweight, also in terms of placement, against the threatening man.

Concluding sentence: Not everything that appears to the eye in a drawing is the message the person who drew it wishes to convey.

The Girl in the Birdcage

THE DRAWING

An 8-year-old girl drew herself in a red dress, inside a cage, or perhaps outside the cage? Above her is a figure with black eyes. Above the cage, a sort of figure appears, a black spirit with very large eyes.

The girl's eyes are also black and opaque, with no detailed pupils.

Up to this point, the description of the drawing seems simple. But the more we return to the drawing, one can discern, with a keen eye, multiple layers.

We will analyze the drawing and its structure by zooming in, diving from the outside in.

Let's look carefully at the original drawing: are you able to see it as a small portion of a person's face?

The upper part of the cage is the nose, the nostrils; the cage is actually the mouth, or more precisely, the large teeth. And the girl is about to be swallowed inside. Such teeth are one of the symbols that characterize a figure associated with violence, and even more so, sexual violence.

For demonstration, I enlarged the original drawing and added eyes so that you can see the face of the hidden figure. Many of you will say, "This is not drawing interpretation. You are adding symbols."

And I say: this is precisely my uniqueness and my method for deciphering drawings of children, adolescents, and families. I enlarge the image; I look for tiny signs with a magnifying glass. Sometimes I embrace the drawing, feel the energies coming from it. I try to understand oil stains or other dirt on the drawing and look for their causes. I search for everything that the subconscious conveyed to the drawing, with the person who drew it as a conduit. In the end, I piece all the signs together into the story of the drawing.

Notice several signs that invite thought and questions.

Is the girl outside the cage?

Perhaps she is inside the cage?

Is there another person with her?

SENSITIVITY AND ETHICS IN ENCOUNTERING VIOLENCE THROUGH CHILDREN'S AND ADOLESCENTS' DRAWINGS

In children's and adolescents' drawings, difficult experiences of violence, harm, or distress are sometimes revealed. The encounter with such drawings obligates the therapist, diagnostician, or educator to act with great sensitivity, professional responsibility, and uncompromising ethics.

Interpretation does not end with identifying graphic signs alone. It requires deep listening to the story behind the drawing, understanding the child's developmental, cultural, and family context, and the ability to distinguish between creative expression and a cry for help.

We will delve into the ethical and emotional considerations required when interpreting drawings that indicate violence, and offer courses of action that combine professionalism, compassion, and caution.

When identifying signs that raise concern, it is important to act with responsibility, discretion, and sound judgment:

- **Do not** ask questions such as: Who did this to you?
- **Do not** rush to draw definitive conclusions – a drawing is only a possible sign.

- **Do** open a conversation with the child in a non-threatening way – "I see you drew something a little sad here... Do you want to tell me about it?"
- **Do** report when there is a reasonable suspicion – in accordance with the legal obligation to report, even if there is no certainty.

WHAT SHOULD WE DO WHEN SUSPICION ARISES?

It is recommended to proceed in stages:

- **Sensitive Information Gathering** – Collect the context of the drawing, engage in dialogue with the child and the parents (if they are not suspected), and ensure accurate documentation.
- **Dialogue with a Multi-Professional Team** – Consult with a counselor, psychologist, or social welfare professional to jointly examine the possibilities.
- **Contacting Authorized Bodies if Necessary** – Sometimes, there is no room for delay due to the fear of ongoing harm.
- **Emotional Follow-up** – Even if there is no unequivocal evidence, the child needs containment, rebuilding of trust, and reconstruction of their sense of security.

PROFESSIONAL BOUNDARIES AND COMMUNICATION WITH EXTERNAL PARTIES

- **Don't remain alone.** The responsibility is shared, it is not yours alone.
- **Do not try to be an investigator, judge, or trauma therapist.**
- **Be a safe address** – Someone who sees, listens, and does not judge.

PRACTICAL EXERCISE WITH CHILDREN AND ADOLESCENTS WHO HAVE EXPERIENCED VIOLENCE AND DRAWN IT

A structured exercise that can serve as a therapeutic, educational, or rehabilitative tool for children harmed by violence, in collaboration with parents, practitioners, law enforcement, and Welfare professionals.

My World: Inside and Outside

OBJECTIVES:

- To enable the child to express feelings, fears, and experiences in a non-threatening way.
- To phrase the prompt according to the drawer's age and the emotional state at the time of the conversation.
- To create a safe space for emotional dialogue.
- To provide a diagnostic tool for professionals.
- To strengthen a sense of control, self-expression, and hope.

Exercise Steps:

1. EMOTIONAL AND ENVIRONMENTAL PREPARATION

Sit in a quiet, pleasant place, with a variety of creative materials: paper, paints, markers, magazine clippings, stickers.

Simple explanation: Today, we will draw your world, as you feel it, and as you want it to be.

2. FIRST DRAWING: MY WORLD NOW

Ask the child to draw the world as it feels right now, at home, at school, in their body, in their heart.

There is no need to be precise or to draw nicely; every mark, color, or shape is correct and valid.

Guiding Questions for the Child Who is Drawing

- Where are you in the drawing?
- Who else is there?
- What is happening there?
- Which colors did you choose, and why?

3. SECOND DRAWING: THE WORLD I WANT

Ask the child to draw a safe, pleasant world where they feel protected, loved, and free.

You may suggest adding symbols of hope, freedom, friends, animals, and favorite places.

Guiding Questions:

- What is different between the drawings?
- What would you like to happen for your world to look like this?

4. ACCOMPANYING EMOTIONAL DIALOGUE

- Do not interpret the drawing; ask open-ended questions.
- Let the child lead the conversation.

- Pay attention to recurring symbols, dark colors, missing or threatening figures.

5. SUMMARY AND EMPOWERMENT

- Emphasize the strengths and positive elements the child expressed in the second drawing.
- Suggest drawing a personal shield, a figure, object, or color that symbolizes protection.
- You can frame the second drawing or keep it in a safe place.

Notes for professionals:

- The exercise is suitable for ages 5-14, with age-appropriate adaptations.
- It should be conducted only with appropriate emotional support.
- Do not force a child to share or explain; the expression itself is what matters, regardless of what is said.
- *It is important to document the process*, with prior consent, of course.

To conclude this not-easy chapter, let's recap the main points. In this section, I added indicators in drawings that can help identify social ostracism.

Summary of Warning Signs in Children's Drawings

These signs may suggest violence (physical/emotional), social ostracism, and sexual abuse.

INDICATORS OF GENERAL VIOLENCE (PHYSICAL/EMOTIONAL)

- Figures with injuries, blood, symbols of violence (fists, weapons, destruction).
- Strong, broken, or unusually dark lines.
- Distorted figures, figures missing body parts (no hands/mouth/eyes).
- A sad, angry, or indifferent facial expression; a solitary figure.
- Figures with empty faces, hollow or dull eyes.
- Scenes of fighting, humiliation, or prominent conflict.
- Signs of avoidance (not drawing figures, drawing only symbols, escaping to unrelated topics).
- The child draws themselves extremely small or floating (a feeling of helplessness or detachment).
- A drawing where the figures are separated by barriers or extreme distance.

INDICATORS OF SOCIAL OSTRACISM/EXCLUSION

- One figure is isolated at the edge of the page, far from the group of figures/children.
- The figures have their backs turned to the isolated figure, or show aggression toward them.
- The drawer does not draw itself at all in a social scene (self-erasure).
- Drawing a group that includes a figure different in appearance, size, or color from the rest.
- A sad, small figure, lacking eye contact, or outside the shared compound.
- Use of dark or cold colors to depict the ostracized figure compared to the colorfulness in the group.
- Scenes of laughter, pointing, mockery, or a single figure expressing a humiliated, weeping expression.

POSSIBLE INDICATORS OF SEXUAL ABUSE

- Emphasis, shading, or erasure of intimate areas on the figure's body: pelvis, mouth, hands, genitals.
- Emphasized lips along with sharp teeth.
- Adult figures with disproportionate body parts: large hands, sharp fingers.
- Absence or clear distortion of organs: mouth, eyes, genitals, sometimes shaded, missing, or appearing identity-less.
- Figures that are unnaturally close or depicted in unusual physical interaction.
- Separation of head from body, or a detached head, hints at traumatic conflict.
- Drawing a small child next to a large or threatening adult clear shows unequal power dynamics.
- Appearance of age-inappropriate symbols or words, especially near the figures.

Please note: a single sign in a drawing usually does not constitute a definitive indication of experiences of violence, ostracism, or sexual abuse; rather, it is grounds for a careful, in-depth review informed by additional knowledge, including clinical assessment. Greater weight is given to identifying recurring patterns, the emotional and developmental context, and overlap with additional emotional or behavioral symptoms.

Clinical assessment is based on cross-referencing drawings, observations, conversations with the child and the surrounding environment, and consultation with relevant professionals when necessary.

TWELVE

DRAWING INTERPRETATION: PROFESSIONAL MODELS

Models Developed from the Field: Therapeutic, Diagnostic, and Educational Approaches Through Drawing

The drawing is not only a product, it is a process.

Through drawing, one can see the psyche in motion, at times resisting, and at times opening anew.

This chapter presents models and approaches for interpreting drawings by children, adolescents, and families.

We will discuss in depth several models that I developed over more than twenty years of work in the field of interpreting drawings by children, adolescents, and families.

The Three Models We Will Focus on Are:

"Family Sits to Draw" - a model centered on a drawing activity with the participation of the entire family. This model can also be used with an entire class or even with a team of employees.

"The Collaborative Drawing" - a structured activity process with the active presence of a facilitator, centered on improving the relationship between two people; parents, siblings, a parent and child, or a pair of friends.

"Projection: From Childhood to Parenthood" - this model enables parents to examine, in a structured way, how their childhood experiences have influenced their parenting patterns. The process of understanding and working through is carried out using a drawing activity as a therapeutic and assessment tool.

MAIN APPROACHES TO INTERPRETING DRAWINGS IN DRAWINGS BY CHILDREN, ADOLESCENTS, AND FAMILIES

Interpreting drawings is a multidisciplinary tool that integrates psychology, art therapy, projective assessment, and developmental observations. Below are several commonly used theoretical and applied approaches:

The Projective-Psychodynamic Approach

- Views the drawing as an *unconscious* expression of conflicts, self-image, and early relationships.
- Focuses on analyzing *symbolic imagery* (tree, house, figures), space, size, colors, lines, erasures, and the placement of elements.
- Examines motifs such as object relations, early distress, and intergenerational transmission.

The Developmental Approach

- Relates to the child's developmental stage and cross-references *graphic maturity* with *emotional and cognitive maturity*.
- Checks whether the ability to draw is consistent with the chronological age, and whether regression to an earlier level has appeared over time.

The Educational-Behavioral Approach

Reflects academic self-image, investment in the task, organization, and thoroughness in the drawing. Emphasizes understanding the links between mobilizing motivation, a sense of belonging or difficulty, and the drawing's nature and content.

Art as Therapy Approach

This approach emphasizes the creative process, not just the product, how the child or adolescent engages artistically: choice of materials, involvement, emotional responses during the work.

The product becomes an *opening for dialogue* and expression, but *is not unequivocal evidence*. It is an invitation to an experiential conversation with the child.

The Family Approach and Interactions

This focuses on family drawings, distances between figures, size and placement, and family roles as reflected in the drawing.

Interpreting the family drawing helps identify feelings of belonging, conflict, power dynamics, and the child's experience of their place within the family system.

The Multi-disciplinary or Integrative Approach

This approach integrates developmental, psychodynamic, cognitive, and social elements, while taking into account cultural, contextual, and environmental aspects. A fundamental principle of this approach is the recognition that no interpretation of a drawing is unambiguous or absolute.

This means that in every interpretive process, one must integrate the findings from the drawing with additional information, such as case history, personal background, and initial observations gathered within the framework of therapy or at school. This combination allows for a multi-dimensional approach that considers the complexity of the child's personal and family experience, the environmental and cultural contexts in which they operate, and information gathered from diverse sources.

KEY PRINCIPLES IN THE INTERPRETATION OF DRAWINGS

- Combine information from as many drawings as possible with additional data (case history, observation, direct conversation with the child/family), and it should never be based solel**y** on a single drawing.
- Symbols and messages are personal and cultural. What signals difficulty for one child in a given culture may be entirely natural for another.

- Observation of repetition, intensity, the types of motifs, and changes *over time* provides a foundation for an accurate professional assessment.
- A professional interpretation process emphasizes listening, close observation, and dialogue with the patient.
- Interpreting drawings is a profound field that combines professional complexity, cultural sensitivity, and the creation of meaningful dialogue between the art and the lived experience of the child, the adolescent, or the family.

MODELS FOR DECODING AND INTERVENTION USING DRAWINGS BY CHILDREN, ADOLESCENTS, AND FAMILIES

DEVELOPING AN ACTION PLAN FOR THE NEXT PHASE OF TREATMENT

After completing the drawing analysis phase and drafting the report, based on integrating information obtained from all sources, including the drawer themself, the parents, welfare professionals, psychologists, family physicians, educators, as well as observations in the educational or home environment, a professional opinion is produced, accompanied by therapeutic recommendations.

The next step in the process is to build a work plan for continued treatment, directly based on the written report and the professional opinion. Ideally, this plan will be a shared, integrative document that combines the recommendations and practical steps proposed by each of the parties involved. In this way, the plan will address the complexity of the case holistically and enable broad coordination and collaboration among all parties, for the benefit of the child and their family.

This is not always possible; the various parties do not always agree. If cooperation is lacking, we proceed to build our plan based on the findings from the drawing analysis, while taking into account the findings of the other parties.

HIERARCHY OF MODELS IN DRAWING INTERPRETATION

The therapeutic process of interpreting drawings is based on three main models, each with a specific purpose and focused use:

The First Model – "Family Sits to Draw"

This model is integrated both in the interpretation phase, to obtain in-depth information about family dynamics, and during the treatment phase as an inseparable part of the work plan. Its purpose is to enable a systemic, broad view of the family as a whole, while incorporating *the personal interpretations of each of its members regarding the same event.*

In this way, we can uncover behavior patterns, interpersonal relationships, feelings, and conflicts within the family, and understand each participant's place and feelings.

The Second Model – "Projection: From Childhood to Parenthood"

This model is designed for focused work with one of the parents in cases where specific difficulties in parental functioning are identified. Using the model, it is possible to identify a difficulty rooted in childhood and to understand how the parents' childhood experiences shape and influence their current parenting. The tool allows for deepening the understanding of past experiences and their impact, leading to a therapeutic process aimed at strengthening parental functioning.

The Third Model – "The Collaborative Drawing "

This model addresses the relationship between two people, in any configuration: parent and child, partners, siblings, cousins, or friends. Its purpose is to examine the nature of the relationship, patterns of communication, the degree of closeness or distance, and the mutual interaction between the two participants. The joint drawing enables a unique view of the interplay in a way that helps identify strengths and challenges and guides the ongoing intervention and treatment.

FAMILY SITS TO DRAW MODEL

A model centered on a drawing activity with the participation of the entire family. This model can also be used when it involves a classroom, and even a group of employees.

The group, or in this case the family, is a closed, dynamic social system in which changes, struggles, and daily challenges take place.

The drawing enables us to understand the outcomes of the intra-group dynamics, from the perspective and understanding of the person who created the drawings.

In the family drawing, we can obtain information about the drawer's attitude toward the home, the family, and society, as well as information about the relationships among family members.

This includes **s**tatuses within the family. Who is closer, who is more distant? Is there a figure that threatens the drawer? Is any family member missing, and why?

The greatest advantage we gain from the *Family Sits to Draw* model is, in fact, the integration of information from each family member. We can see and learn how *each* family member interprets the same event.

CASE STUDY

A family, mother, father, and three children, two sons and one daughter among them. The relationship between the father and one of the children: the father leaves for work early in the morning before the children have woken up, and returns home in the afternoon. The older son, after a few minutes with the father and the family, goes into his room and does his homework. Although the atmosphere at home is good, loving, and very close, the older son chooses not to be with the family during the hours when the father comes home.

The parents approached me about the case; after a discussion, we decided to proceed in two ways: first, interpreting drawings by the older son; the second path, to use the "Family Sits to Draw" model.

By combining the information, we can identify where the reason for the older son's deliberate distance is revealed, what needs to be addressed, and who is the source of the reason the child is withdrawing.

In the child's drawing, signs of physical closeness to the father emerged. Through the family drawing, it is possible to understand that the child interprets the parents' relationship as distant.

In light of the child's drawing, I recommended to the parents that they use the "Family Sits to Draw" model in order to reveal what is really going on with the child and why he behaves in a withdrawn way.

We will return to the case later...

FAMILY SITS TO DRAW - STRUCTURE OF THE MODEL AND ITS STAGES.

The stages:

1. Introductory conversation with a parent/parents.
2. Initial joint drawing session for the entire family.
3. Interpretation of the drawings, identifying areas of friction or areas that need treatment.
4. Conversation with the parents and submission of the report.
5. A concluding drawing session together with all family members. It is recommended and desirable to bring the previous drawings to the session to examine the changes that occurred through the process.

According to the results, we submit a *family* work plan, based on the understanding and perspective that every solution must be addressed with the entire family; every action we take, or improvement we achieve, will affect the whole family.

Introductory Conversation with a Parent/Parents

The introductory meeting with the parents usually takes place following a difficulty the child is experiencing or a troubling drawing. In rare cases, the first meeting is held with the whole family, usually after a referral from a professional who knows the model and the family background. In such cases, initial information is also received from the referring party.

Assuming we have already passed the family's initial drawing stage, in the meeting, I explain to the parents the family drawing process, the objectives, and the aim of the joint drawings to the parents.

THE QUESTION OF DECEPTION IN THE PROCESS OF INTERPRETING FAMILY DRAWINGS

A question that often comes up from parents is: "What is the logic in the parents knowing the purpose of the drawing? After all, they can try to mislead the interpreter by means of a staged drawing that does not reflect reality as it is." This is a legitimate concern, since the parents' awareness of the aims of the process could, ostensibly, allow them to influence the results of the interpretation.

Dealing with the Possibility of Deception

The main advantage of the model is that it is based on different points of view from each of the participants regarding the same family situation. Even if a parent tries to "fool" the interpreter, the process itself reveals additional data from the subconscious through the drawing, even when it is deliberate or "fake." Combined with the information obtained from the rest of the family members, the chances of deception drop significantly.

Beyond that, the interpreter's professional responsibility is to consider the drawings as a whole and to identify unusual data, recurring patterns, or signs indicating an attempt at deception. Therefore, the integrity of the process is maintained, despite the theoretical possibility of deception.

Since we draw things from the subconscious, a "fake" drawing will still contain additional data that clarifies the true picture. Combined with the additional information from the other family members, the chances of deception are very low.

Joint Drawing Sessions with the Entire Family

We hold at least two drawing sessions with the family. If worrisome signs arise, an additional, smaller session is held with at least three participants. I initiate this when there is suspicion of domestic violence.

First Family Session

THE DRAWING ENVIRONMENT IN THE FIRST SESSION

The drawing environment is a central component in the success of the family's first session. Creating a pleasant and comfortable atmosphere is a necessary condition, as the goal of the activity is for all family members to draw together, not each one separately in their own room. The physical closeness between participants increases excitement and emotions during the drawing and helps stimulate the subconscious. Cooperation and mutual presence create a rich family dynamic that is beneficial to the diagnostic process.

THE IMPORTANCE OF OBSERVATION AND SITTING TOGETHER

As part of my work, I integrate observation as an inseparable component of the session. To that end, it is important that all family members sit close to one another, preferably around a large table. This setup allows comfortable and effective observation, and also increases interaction among family members. The ability to see and listen to interactions in real time provides rich, in-depth information about the family relationship system and enriches the professional process.

For the same observational reasons, I prefer that the box of colors be placed at the center of the room or the table where the drawing is taking place. It is possible to divide the materials into two boxes of colors. Since the age range is wide, it is advisable to provide coloring and writing tools of various kinds, including crayons, oil pastels, pencils, in a range of colors, including black, as well as a regular graphite pencil.

Beyond that, to create a pleasant, enjoyable experience, you can incorporate music, or food, anything that helps everyone settle into a relaxed mood.

Prepare in advance drawing sheets of at least A4 size paper, and give each participant one sheet at the start of each task. This preserves the information, with all changes and erasures on the same sheet, without the option to replace it. You can use the bottom of a plate, cardboard, or a book as a drawing surface, and if needed, you may hand out several sheets; at the end of each topic, collect the sheets that were used and leave only blank sheets for the next part of the work. If an additional sheet is added for each drawing, keep them together for assessment purposes, or mark, for example, on the back of the drawing "Tree 1," "Tree 2."

The order of subjects to draw will be somewhat different from an individual assessment, because we are engaged in a family process. Therefore, we will ask the family to draw on subjects in the following order:

- Tree
- Animal
- Figure
- House
- Family

Since we are working with a larger number of people, we will make an effort to keep closer to the time for each drawing, but without stating it directly and without setting limits in advance. We will move along with the process; this is an excellent opportunity to observe the balance of power and family dominance.

As noted, at the end of each stage, we collect all the drawings. Only if the person who drew did not write their name on the sheet will we ask their permission to write their name on the back of the drawing.

The Questioning Stage

In the "Family Sits to Draw" model, the questioning stage is complex. I usually avoid direct questioning. I glance at the drawings while the next drawing stage is underway. If I notice something that "requires" clarification, I do so within earshot of the group, in a kind of privacy, mainly for the children, to create a safe space. This allows them to give a truthful answer without fear of one kind or another. If questions arise during the interpretation itself, I write them down and save them for the second meeting or initiate a meeting with the drawer, all depending on the urgency of the information I perceive.

The Interpretation Stage

The interpretation process takes a long time. It is also more complex, both because of the number of drawings and participants, and because of the need to compare information between those who drew.

If I immediately identify any violence, I speed up the pace of interpretation because of the urgency of the matter.

Writing the interpretation report is also more complex: each participant receives a separate report, followed by a joint report for everyone.

We present the report's conclusions in another meeting with the parents, including conclusions and recommendations for continued treatment.

Returning to the Case Description from Page 183

In interpreting the boy's drawings, he would shut himself in his room after his father returned from work, which led to an initial hypothesis, even before the drawings were submitted, that the boy was likely afraid of his father for some reason.

Looking at the drawings, physical violence was ruled out; the boy drew his father close to him and held his hand. In the family drawing, I noticed that the boy drew the parents far from one another, and I understood that, from the boy's point of view, the relationship between his parents was not good. Therefore, I recommended entering the "Family Sits to Draw" model.

During the family drawing meeting, through observation, I was able to see several things even before I arrived at interpreting the drawings. The boy sat far from his parents, who sat next to each other, and moreover, he sat with his back turned to his parents.

The drawing activity lasted about an hour.

Because of the prior information I received from the parents about the boy's behavior, and the findings from the family drawing the boy drew, I focused my observation on the boy's behavior, specifically during the drawing of the family and the house. There I sensed the boy's discomfort; he bent over the drawing as if trying to hide it.

When I looked at the two drawings during the interpretation, two particularly salient elements stood out.

In the house drawing, one can see that all the windows of the house are dark. Note that this is during daylight hours; only one window on the second floor is lit. Checking with the parents, I understood that this is the boy's room. This explains the fact that the boy is in his room. This is a *relatively reassuring* finding because the boy sees his room as a positive, good place; he feels comfortable there. It would be more concerning if the situation were the opposite, if the window of his room were dark.

In the family drawing, there was a small surprise. The boy drew a close family experience; his parents are close in the drawing, and the communication is calm and pleasant. But note that the boy is behind, not in the family circle, yet he is touching his father, and his gaze is toward his mother. Here, too, it is relatively reassuring compared with the family drawing he drew earlier.

When I examined the family drawings of the other family members, in all of them, without exception, there was a warm, close family experience. In all the drawings, the boy is in the center, so everyone experiences his presence positively.

In light of the data, I decided to sit separately with the boy, together with the drawings, to listen to his explanations.

Regarding the house drawing, I asked:

"Whose house is it?"

"Whose room is the one with the light on?"

"Why is there light only there?"

"Did you forget the light on in the room?"

In the family drawing, the goal was to understand the child's position; although he is the eldest, he is relatively small, slightly behind, touching his father, and looking toward his mother.

"What a nice, loving family, whose family is this?"

"Can you tell me who everyone is?"

"What do you feel right now, do you feel comfortable with everyone in the drawing?"

“What is bothering you?”

"What is Dad saying to everyone?"

Then I introduced the following sentence into the conversation: "How nice that father and mother love each other so much."

I noticed his eyes shifting sideways. "Yeah, real fun." We continued the conversation, and gradually, more details emerged and came together. The child experiences the dialogue between father and mother as power struggles, from which he recoils; he experiences them as arguing loudly. He is apprehensive and, therefore, prefers to be in his room, where it is quiet, and he feels safe.

When I examined the rest of the family drawings, I did not find signs that corresponded to what he said. Increasingly, I considered the possibility that this was, in fact, a difficulty in auditory sensory regulation, which causes him to experience the dialogue between the parents as a fight. This leads him to go into his room, and in this way, he "quiets" their exchange.

I recommended that the parents have a hearing test done, try to speak near the child at lower volumes, and perhaps even whisper between themselves. And, where possible, increase physical touch between them in the child's presence in order to strengthen his sense that all is well between them.

THE IMPACT OF AUDITORY SENSORY REGULATION DIFFICULTY ON THE CHILD AND FAMILY DYNAMICS

As the process continued, it became clear that the child was dealing with a difficulty in auditory sensory regulation, which explained his reaction to the family dynamic and to the loud discourse between the parents. The parents' physical closeness, emphasized in the child's presence, served as a source of soothing for him and reduced the sense of threat and tension he experienced due to the power struggles and loud exchanges between the parents.

The positive effect of the physical closeness not only calmed the child but also increased the closeness between the parents themselves. Gradually, the child began to feel more at ease within the family framework and started spending more time with all family members, which contributed to an improved sense of security and harmony at home.

THE COLLABORATIVE DRAWING MODEL

The Collaborative Drawing model has been well known for many years. The version presented here includes updates and changes made to adapt and integrate it to drawing-interpretation work.

A Brief Explanation

THE COMPLEXITY OF RELATIONSHIPS AND COPING THROUGH A COLLABORATIVE DRAWING

Relationships between two people, whether a child with an adult, a child with a child, or an adult with an adult, form a complex arena in which emotions, personal interpretations, power struggles, domineering behavior, and sometimes concessions intertwine. Within the family, turbulent dynamics often develop; for example, a charged relationship between a father and his son. Components such as ego, power struggles, and past burdens can serve as fertile ground for continuous struggles and friction.

Through the process of collaborative drawing, it becomes possible to reach the "treatment points", those sensitive places that pose a challenge in the relationship. This activity helps take down walls and face the challenges, thereby stabilizing a calm, respectful, and enabling relationship. Improving the relationship between a father and son, for example, ultimately leads to reduced tensions and a sense of stability in the family's overall relationships.

THE STAGES IN THE COLLABORATIVE DRAWING MODEL

The activity is carried out between two participants in the presence of a facilitator, whose role is essential to the success of the process. The facilitator may be a parent who has undergone appropriate training, a social worker, or a licensed therapist. The facilitator must ensure that the workspace remains respectful, enabling, and free of verbal or physical violence. The facilitator's central task is to maintain a safe atmosphere and monitor the dynamics between the participants throughout the process.

During the stages of the activity, the facilitator should stay alert to what is happening and pay attention to the interaction between the two participants. The role also includes intervening with trigger questions; questions intended to lead the participants to address points of friction and examine their relationship in situations of struggle, power, lack of compassion, or communication difficulties. These questions help deepen the process and create opportunities for open and honest dialogue on issues essential to the relationship.

The facilitator's approach throughout all stages of the meeting is enabling, sensitive, and respectful. The goal is to guide the participants to face personal and interpersonal challenges, and to create a space in which it is possible to deal with difficulties and build a healthy, balanced relationship.

THE STAGES:

A Preliminary Conversation with Both Participants

In the preliminary conversation, the facilitator explains and details the process, its goals, and the stages one after another, especially the practical stages in the process of collaborative drawing process.

Preparing the Space and Tools

The workspace should be comfortable and pleasant for drawing; you can draw on the table or on the floor. The recommended drawing sheet size is **A2** or as large as possible, not an A4 sheet. If a large sheet is not available, join together four A4 sheets. Place one box with a wide range of colors in the center of the drawing sheet so that both participants can easily reach it, and so it will be sufficiently "complex" to elicit situations of "friction" and dialogue.

The facilitator sits at some distance from the drawing area; if the room is small, then as far away as possible. It is also recommended to prepare a comfortable place for the facilitator to write.

Stage of Dividing the Page into Two Equal Parts

Dividing the page into two parts is very important for two main reasons: to create "my area" and "your area," which can create points of "friction" between the participants; and due to the need to create distance between each participant's drawing, so that we can connect them together in the next stage of the process. One can fold the page in half and then open it and draw, or one can draw a broken line with a pencil to divide it.

Each Person Draws a Free Drawing in Their Designated Half of the Page

At this stage, the subject is freely chosen; each person draws what feels right to them. From my experience, even at this stage, both sides draw something related to the reason we have gathered. Although we do not restrict the drawing area within each one's half, try, both in your explanation and during the drawing stage, to ask them to draw as close to the center of their half as possible.

At the End of the Drawing, Each Person Outlines and Encircles the Drawing They Made.

If you drew a temporary dividing line in pencil, now is the time to erase it. Each person surrounds their drawing in this way, as in the example.

Creating a Bridge Between the Two Drawings, Each in a Free Form

Now each participant, as guided by the facilitator, connects the two drawings to one another with a line (a bridge) and decorates the bridge in any way they see fit.

A Collaborative Drawing on All the Remaining Area of the Sheet

The participants decide together on the subject, and in the drawing, each one draws their part, with interaction between the two drawers. This time, the subject is determined in advance by both drawers; they *must* reach an agreement on the subject of the drawing. Each person may draw wherever they wish, *not inside the previously delimited drawing.*

Deciding on a Title for the Collaborative Drawing

The two participants need to decide on a title *together* and explain why they chose the selected title. Write the chosen title in a location agreed upon jointly, and decorate the title together.

Summary Conversation of the Activity

When you finish the drawing activity, hang the joint drawing on the wall and sit facing it to hold a conversation, led by the facilitator. This is not yet the final conversation, because we may conduct another session later, and only then will we hold a concluding conversation, which is usually with the parents without the child. There, we present proposals for next steps.

The Results

There is no absolute metric for success one way or the other; it is not black and white. Success is measured over time by changes in the behavior and relationship of the two participants and, likewise, by longer-term changes in the overall behavior of the entire family unit.

In this drawing, you can see that the work here does not follow the model's rules; you can see two worlds and different messages. The reason for this outcome is that a dynamic between the two began immediately. I preferred to continue with the dynamic that had developed and kept flowing, so there was no need to create the personal spaces in order to generate the triggers, it was simply there. By the end of the session, practically all the barriers in the interpersonal communication between the two had been removed.

PROJECTION: FROM CHILDHOOD TO PARENTHOOD MODEL

A model that examines with the parents what and how their childhood influences who they are today as parents.

PROJECTION: FROM CHILDHOOD TO PARENTHOOD

In interpreting drawings by children, adolescents, and families, we focus on two primary drawings that provide information about one parent's childhood experiences: the house drawing and the family drawing. These drawings allow us to look at memories tied to the childhood home and family in the past, alongside the home and family in the present, when that person has already become a parent.

Central Questions in the Interpretation Process

Over the years, many questions have arisen from parents about the nature of the drawings they create. In the interpretation session, the parent may be asked to draw their childhood home and specify all the components and memories connected to it. Next, the parent is asked to draw their family as they experienced it in childhood. In the following stage, the parent draws the home in which they live today and their family in the present. In this way, we obtain two significant points in time, the past and the present, that enable us to examine the mutual influence between childhood experiences and current parenting behavior.

The Model: Projection: From Childhood to Parenthood

The Projection: From Childhood to Parenthood model is intended to help understand how childhood experiences in one's family of origin affect current parenting behavior. The ability to work in parallel on past and present allows deep learning and the ability to make adjustments in parenting behavior for the sake of the present and the family's future.

The Emotional Aspect of the Process

This is a complex emotional process, in which the parent is called to delve into personal memories, return to childhood days, and to events that shaped them as a child, an adolescent, and an adult. Opening old wounds is especially challenging when there were difficult experiences, such as violence, which require deep emotional work during the interpretation process.

Hardship grows in the dark, more and more; when exposed to light, it loses its power until it disappears.

STAGES OF THE MODEL

1. An opening conversation in the clinic with the parent in question.
2. Creating the childhood-period drawings.
3. A conversation to analyze and interpret the drawings. The parent who draws is the one who deciphers the drawings, together with the drawing interpreter. All the information the parent provides is recorded. *The drawing interpreter does not intervene at all at the interpretation stage.*
4. An open conversation with the parent about the issues; at this stage, the drawing interpreter adds their own interpretation of the drawing.

This is done twice: with the family drawing and with the house drawing.

AFTER A REFRESHMENT BREAK

1. Creating the drawings, the family and the house in the present, by the parent.
2. The parent interprets or explains the drawings while we record the interpretation.
3. A conversation and interpretation by the interpreter, together with the parent, about the differences between the past drawings and the

present drawings. If there are differences, what are they?
4. How does the parent see the difference between the drawings?
5. Does the parent recognize overlap between their own behaviors and those of their parents?
6. How does this affect the way they relate to or raise their children?

IN THE SUMMARY MEETING

INVOLVING THE CHILD IN THE SUMMARY MEETING – PRINCIPLES AND GUIDELINES

There are cases in which it is appropriate to involve the child in the summary meeting, particularly when the parent recognizes and understands the need to do so. In these situations, a joint drawing deciphering session takes place between the parent and the child or children. During this session, an open dialogue is held about the experience of parenthood from the child's perspective: what they feel, whether they would like to change things, and so on.

This session is possible only when there is complete openness between parent and child. In addition, it is important to ensure that the child has high emotional intelligence and the ability to process the deep conversation that is likely to take place. These requirements apply equally to the parent, since the success of the meeting depends on both sides' ability to be open, attentive, and willing to share.

At the end of the process, the work done is internal, personal, and intensive, a process of learning lessons, emotional processing, and changing one's way of life.

THIRTEEN

PRACTICING THE INTERPRETATION OF DRAWINGS BY CHILDREN, ADOLESCENTS, AND FAMILIES

It is time for some interpretation challenges; let's practice together

"Knowledge is acquired through learning; professionalism is forged through repeated practice, where each attempt builds a layer of skill until the whole exceeds the sum of its parts."

EXPLANATION FOR THE PRACTICE CHAPTER

Over the course of the journey we have taken together around interpreting drawings, we have reached the stage where we actually practice the principles learned. Along the way, we paused at key points to understand certain drawings in depth and consider how to approach them. Now, we focus on interpreting a drawing step by step, and apply the knowledge we acquired in previous lessons.

The Importance of Practice and Experience

The essential difference between a good professional and an excellent one lies in the quantity and quality of practice and experience. The more one practices, the more focused and efficient the interpretation processes become. Experience allows us to distinguish essence from peripheral details, to know how to approach a drawing, and to interpret it accurately and deeply.

Methods and the Uniqueness of the Approach

In the world of drawing interpretation, there are many approaches and diverse methods, as we discussed earlier. However, the method presented here was built from personal experience, continual learning, and daily practice. It is a method that has been taking shape from day one, in motion, through experience and learning, and it enables anyone to develop the skill and professionalism required to interpret drawings.

USING INTUITION AS A TOOL IN INTERPRETING DRAWINGS

One of the central and significant tools in the process of interpreting drawings is the interpreter's personal intuition. Some professionals choose to ignore intuition, but here we place clear emphasis on its importance in the interpretation process. The recommendation is not to fear intuition, but to use it with awareness and attentiveness, to ensure that it does not sway the interpreter emotionally and that objectivity and freedom from external influences are maintained.

Why is Intuition Essential in Interpreting Drawings?

The drawing itself is a deep emotional expression; the person who draws brings into it sensations, thoughts, and emotional places that are sometimes in the subconscious. When viewing a drawing, intuition enables the interpreter to connect with the inner world of the person who drew it, their feelings, their difficulties, and even their heart and mind. Thus, an opportunity is created to "live" the drawer's experience from the perspective they wish to share, and to deepen the under standing of the story behind the drawing.

In conclusion, intuition is not just an auxiliary tool, it is a vital gateway to understanding the emotion and experience conveyed through the drawing, as long as professional objectivity is maintained in the interpretation process.

DRAWING INTERPRETATION FORM, AN AID IN THE INTERPRETATION WORK

I recommend that you write down everything about the drawing, really everything. I still do this today.

When it is written down, it remains, and you can return to this data at any stage. The items in the table are examples of what can be recorded, drawn from experience over the years.

Drawing Interpretation Form

Name of the person drawing____________. Referring party__________. Date:____________.

Random drawing: yes/no From a process: yes/ no Total number of drawings:_____. Age of the person drawing:____.

Theme of the drawing:__________________________________.

Feature/Field	**Example Data/Observations**
Colors in the Drawing	Red, Green, Black, Orange
Prominent Symbols	Dog, Cross, Sharp objects, Broken window
Events in the Drawing	Child sitting on the side while a group of children is playing; Woman lying on the floor with two soldiers standing over her; Broken heart in orange inside a transparent box; Man sitting on the side watching children play in the neighborhood garden.

Feature/Field	Example Data/Observations
Coloring Style	Pleasant and soft; Short lines in the shape of lightning bolts; Straight lines, sharp angles; Very thick lines
People in the Drawing	An additional person in the family; A missing person in the family; Number of people around; Children or adults
Types of Trees in the Drawing	Tall tree with a pointed crown; Tall tree, thick trunk, many branches, leaves, and fruits; Tree with a thin and small trunk, crown without leaves; Tree with a thick trunk, near the crown of the tree there is a spiral wound

Feature/Field	Example Data/Observations
General Description of the Drawing	Isolated house on a hill, above the mountain on the left side is a red sun without rays. Above the hill, a flock of birds flies toward the right; Zoo with many animals, some in cages, some free. On the left side there is a restaurant, two people are standing in front of the restaurant; Bed in the forest, near the bed stands a man with a beard. The man has one long hand and one short hand. A cat with a human face is lying on the bed; A large forest with different types of trees, there is a group of cypress-like trees, a group of trees with a very large canopy, some of the trees with leaves, some with fruits.
Repeating Shapes	Triangles, Arrows, Ladders, Bicycles

Feature/Field	Example Data/Observations
My Intuition Regarding the Drawing	Difficult atmosphere of fear; Loving and happy family; Suspicion of sexual violence; Anxieties
My Finding (from drawing information only)	In the drawing, the child tells us about the difficulty and fear of his father; he draws the father in the family drawing as a giant with very large hands. The only window lit in the dark house explains to us that there is a point of light in the house for the drawer. The child suffers from abandonment anxiety. Most likely due to the father's condition, the child feels insecurity.

Feature/Field	Example Data/Observations
Information from the Referring Party	Divorced parents, children live one week with the father and one week with the mother; The child underwent a psycho-didactic assessment, and it was found that... The child is being treated by a therapist and a Chinese acupuncturist; The father was injured in a car accident and remains restricted.
Does the Drawing Reinforce Previous Information?	Yes, in the kindergarten drawing, he draws a violent child, most likely suffering from violence. No, according to the drawing, there seems to be no repetition in the drawings. Yes, the child places himself in the family drawing close to the father, who is sitting in a wheelchair.

Feature/Field	Example Data/Observations
Finding and Recommendation for Next Steps	Conversation with a social worker, referral for parent and family guidance; Recommend entering a drawing interpretation process based on the model of the family sitting down to draw; In my opinion, there is a barrier in the relationship between the siblings, I recommend a joint drawing activity.
Words Written on the Drawing	Mom, Dad, and I; Stop it; It hurts me; Why?
What the Child Said About the Drawing	That's Dad; A small monster that protects me; Dad's knife; Sometimes Mom shouts
Things I Want to Add Myself	Any additional things you find important to write in the table; You are also invited to update colleagues in the WhatsApp group; New things you think are suitable for your working method.

GUIDELINES FOR A CONVERSATION WITH THE CHILD REGARDING THE DRAWING

When having a conversation with the child about their drawing, it is highly recommended to be fully present throughout the process, especially when the conversation is pre-planned. The adult's full attention helps the child feel safe and open up to the discussion.

Be sure to write the child's words on a separate sheet of paper, not on the drawing itself. Alternatively, you can ask the child for permission to make a copy of the drawing before the interview, and if the child agrees, you may write notes on the copy rather than on the original drawing.

It is very important to maintain personal space, respect, and interest toward the child. This approach gives the child a sense of safety and allows them to cooperate more easily during the conversation.

USING THE TABLE AS A WORKING TOOL

The table presented here has served as a central working tool for over twenty years. All information is gathered and consolidated on a single page, and each drawing has a separate page. This way, you can return to review information collected in the past and integrate information from different sources when preparing the final report.

It is very important that you remember: there is no such thing as right or wrong in what you see!!!

What you see is the right thing. It is quite possible that another interpreter will see different things and draw different conclusions, and that is also correct. What matters is that, in the end, we connect all the information into conclusions and recommendations that come together into an appropriate and effective work plan.

GUIDELINES FOR WORKING WITH AND ANALYZING DRAWINGS

Presenting and Comparing the Drawings

During the analysis process, drawings are presented, sometimes even two similar ones side by side, to allow comparison and deepen understanding. Alongside each drawing, questions and hints are presented, intended to help and guide you into the way of thinking I employ. The questions and guidance are intended to expand the observation and deepen the understanding.

Recording Observations and Drawing Details

It is recommended to use a dedicated table or a sheet of paper and write down everything you notice in the drawing, without exception. Emphasis should also be placed on details that may seem unimportant, as their significance sometimes becomes clear only at later stages. It is important to rely at least on the elements recommended in the table to ensure a full and in-depth observation.

Writing Conclusions and Recommendations

Upon completion of the observation, you must formulate your conclusions and recommendations from the analysis in a few lines. These conclusions will support the next steps and serve as a basis for professional, focused work.

Referring to the Appendices and Personal Interpretation

In the appendices at the end of the book, you will find my personal interpretation, opinions, and recommendations for next steps. It is recommended not to read the interpretation in advance, but to go through the process yourself, out of trust in the learning process.

The Importance of Personal Observation

Do not rush to look for a "right answer" in the material. Write down everything that comes to mind, even if it seems, at first glance, illogical, since every observation is legitimate. It is important to remember there is no right or wrong; the goal is to integrate all the information from the drawings, the professionals, the family, and the person drawing, in order to reach a complete, in-depth understanding.

Getting Started

The journey begins here; observe, record, draw conclusions, and do not hesitate to think creatively and originally. Any information collected will contribute to the overall picture and to the professional process.

DRAWING NO. 1: THE HOUSE WITH THE OPEN DOOR

Hints: the door, the tree, the chimney, the path.

Recommendations: Try to think about what each clue is saying. Try to relate two hints to each other and see whether they share a common message.

- Why is there no smoke from the chimney?
  What might that say?

- To which side did the door open, and why is it located on this side in particular?
- The tree: where is it placed?
- What is the meaning of the house's interior color?

DRAWING NO. 2: PLAYING IN THE PARK

Hints: a tree, the last child in the group, a distant child, the figure that is very far away.

Recommendations: Pay attention to the situation, to all the participants, and to the distances between them.

- Why does the tree look like this? What message might it carry?

- Try to think: who drew this picture?
- Who is the leader in the group of children? Why?
- What is happening to the child under the tree?

DRAWING NO. 3: THE ADULT, THE CHILD, AND THE STRING

Hints: the background, the child's eyes, the string, the adult's eyes.

Recommendations: Try to think about what each clue is saying. Try to refer to two hints together and see whether they share a common message.

- What is under the adult's eyes? What might that suggest?
- The relative size of the child and the adult?

- What is the significance of the string, rope, or chain?
- The adult's groin area?

DRAWING NO. 4: THE PARENTS, THE JUDGING GIRL

Hints: the girl, the situation, the feet.

Recommendations: Try to think about what the girl's placement tells us. Try to refer to two hints together and see whether they share a common message.

- The movement of each person's legs, what might that say?
- What are they talking about?
- The girl, what does the placement indicate?
- The adults' hands, what do they tell?

DRAWING NO. 5: LOVE WITH A SPOT ON THE FOREHEAD

Hints: the situation, the child's eyes, the spot on the forehead, the nose.

Recommendations: Try to consider the child's size and placement. The size of the head and the size of the neck.

- What is the central message in the drawing?
- The shape of the spot on the forehead, what can be understood from it?
- The size relationships between the children and the child in the center?
- The direction of the eyes of *each one* of those present, what is the meaning?

DRAWING NO. 6: THE ENTRANCE TO DARKNESS

Hints: the colors, the gaze, the blue frame.

Recommendations: Try to think about what the blue frame says as a message.

- What is the central message in the drawing?
- What is the meaning of the difference between the background inside the frame and the background outside the frame?
- The red cheeks, do they connect to the central message, and how?
- The gaze: what do you feel when you look at the gaze and the eyes?

DRAWINGS NO. 7 AND 8: THE BIRDS ON THE TREE

Notice that the situation is very similar; you could say the same situation.

- What is the difference in the drawing's story?
- In the proximity of the house in each drawing?
- The bird's placement, its direction?
- Height in the tree, proximity to the house?

DRAWING NO. 8

- Notice the fruit on the floor. What could that hint at?
- What is the meaning of the bench next to the house?
- Why is it empty?
- What is the meaning of the house's color?

DRAWING NO. 9: SUN OVER THE GREEN SEA

Hints: Pay attention to... the sun's size and placement; size relationships among the sun, the child, and the mountains.

Questions:

- What do the sun's rays tell us?
- What is the meaning of the rays' sizes and shades?
- Why does the child turn his back to the sun?
- What comes to mind when you look at the ground beneath the child's feet?

DRAWING NO. 10: EATING AND ENJOYING

Hints: Pay attention to... the tree's posture, the door's direction.

Questions:

- What might the girl's "third leg" symbolize?
- What kind of communication is there between the children?
- The missing leg of the table on the boy's side, what could that tell?
- The number of handles on the front door!

DRAWING NO. 11: SUN, WARM OR COLD?

Hints: Pay attention to the sun's size and placement; size relationships among the sun, the child, and the mountains.

Questions:

- What do the sun's rays tell us?
- The child's gaze toward the sun, what is the meaning?
- Try to look at the sun's rays in two ways: once the yellow rays, and once focus on the orange color as rays. If you managed to notice, what difference, if any, is there in your interpretation?

DRAWING NO. 12: EATING AND ENJOYING 2

Hints: Pay attention to the number of trees and their placement, the distance of the table from the house.

Questions:

- What might the sun symbolize? Try to interpret the relationship with the mother?
- What is the relationship between the children?
- What is the meaning of the gray color on the roof, the windows, and the door?
- What is the meaning of the handle's color, and how does it connect to the gray?

DRAWING NO. 13: THE MAN AND THE KNIFE 1

Two drawings of a man with a knife, do the two drawings assign the same meaning to the knife?

Hints: Pay attention to the colors versus the message, what is the meaning?

Questions:

- What is the meaning of the beard and the spot under the chin?
- Where are the figure's eyes looking?
- What is the difference in the way the knife is held, compared to the grip in the second drawing?
- The background, the clouds, how do they compare with the figure's colors?

- Try to connect with your intuition about the situation.

DRAWING NO. 14: THE MAN AND THE KNIFE 2

Hints: Pay attention to the two background colors.

Questions:

- Where is the adult who is holding the knife looking?
- Are the two drawings with the knife truly identical in their message?
- Here too, pay attention to how the knife is held.
- Where is the person holding the knife looking in this drawing?

- Do you get the same feeling from both drawings?

DRAWING NO. 15: MOTHER? GIRL?

Hints: Pay attention to ages, pregnancy, baby, and mother

Questions:

- What can the gaze of the sun tell us?
- Is the girl holding a baby or a doll?
- Is she holding the doll, or a baby?
- Consider the age of the pregnant woman.
- What is the meaning of the girl with her back to the sun?

DRAWING NO. 16: FAMILY ON THE MOVE

Hints: Pay attention to the girl in purple, the father, and the clothing.

Questions:

- What does the father's gaze toward the child in green tell us?
- What does the mother's body posture tell us?
- Notice the difference between the direction of the mother's body and the direction of her eyes. What does it mean?
- What do we learn about the family's relationships?
- Who is the dominant figure in the family?

DRAWING NO. 17: TRIANGLE OF ANIMALS IN DIALOGUE

Hints: Pay attention to the situation, the participants.

Questions:

- Is there a connection between the animals' traits and the situation?
- What is the meaning of each animal's trait for the situation?
- What does the dog's color tell us about the topic of the conversation?
- Try to map the animals to people.
- What is the dog's role?

DRAWING NO. 18: CONVERSATION BETWEEN FRIENDS?

Hints: Pay attention to the background, the figures' placement, and size.

Questions:

- The figure on the right, what do the legs tell us?
- The direct eye gaze, what does it tell us about their relationship?
- What do you think about the situation, positive or negative?

DRAWING NO. 19: THE SIBLINGS, AT HOME?

Hints: Pay attention to the children's positions, the window's structure.

Questions:

- The gaze of the child on the left, what can it tell us?
- What does the children's physical location tell us about their emotional position?
- Pay close attention: Are the children inside the house or outside?
- Try to imagine the story of the case in your mind!
- Connect with one of the figures, whom did you connect with?

- What do you feel toward the figure you did not choose to be?

DRAWING NO. 20: TOWER OF PRIDE

Hints: Pay attention to the tower's location and size, colors as a message, the tower's shape

Questions:

- What is the meaning of the tower's windows? When were they drawn?
- What is the meaning of the trees?
- What is the meaning of the shape of the tower's roof? Is there a connection to the colors on the tower?
- The red sun, what does it tell us?

- Pay attention to the movement in the background and try to integrate that with your thoughts about the tower. What comes up for you?

DRAWING NO. 21: GRAY SMOKE AND THE BLUE?

Hints: Pay attention to the smoke, the sky-blue patch, and the number of chimneys.

Questions:

- What does the intensity of the smoke teach us?
- How do you feel about the sky-blue patch in the sky?
- What is the meaning of the second chimney? Why is there no smoke?

- What is the connection between the color of the smoke from the chimney and the colors reflected from inside the house?

DRAWING NO. 22: THE THREE CROSSES

Hints: Pay attention to the hue/shade, the crosses, the path, and the figure.

Questions:

- What is the meaning of the long path?
- What is the meaning of the crosses?
- What do you think is the story behind the drawing?
- What do you feel about the child's physical condition?

- What is the significance of the child's walking direction? Does it have meaning for the whole story?

DRAWING NO. 23: THE STORM, RIGHT AND LEFT

Hints: Pay attention to the tree's unusual structure, the directions of pressure

Questions:

- What feeling do you get from the tree's unusual structure?
- The directions of pressure on the tree?
- What is the meaning of the drawing's color?
- Do you recognize any figure in the drawing?

- After your interpretation of the drawing, give it a name that reflects your interpretation!

DRAWING NO. 24: THE BROKEN WINDOW!

Hints: Pay attention to windows, path, chimney

Questions:

- Do you notice a slope on the roof? In which direction?
- What is the significance of the slope?
- What is the connection between the shape of the roof (the slope) and the state of the left window?
- What is the meaning of the path and its shape?

- Why, in your opinion, is there a difference between the shape of the windows on the left and the right window?

DRAWING NO. 25: THE LONG NECK, WHY?

Hints: Pay attention to eyes, neck, and shading.

Questions:

- The structure of the eyes? Where is the gaze positioned?
- The meaning of the neck's length?
- What is the significance of the chin's shading? What might it teach us?
- Could the squint be related to the shading on the chin?

- What do you feel about the adolescent's condition?
- Do you think he is in any kind of dilemma?

DRAWING NO. 26: THE CHILD ON THE ROOF!

Hints: Pay attention to the child on the roof, the figure in the house, and the colors.

Questions, hints:

- The child on the roof, why is he there? What is he looking for up there?
- What is the connection between the roof's color and the shirt of the figure inside the house?

- What is the meaning of the house's color and the color of the little child's shirt?
- The sun in the drawing, explain: what is its connection to the child on the roof?

CONCLUSIONS

To sum up, only after you have completed your interpretation, go to the solutions section and check yourselves: is your interpretation close to mine?

If not, check why?

Repeat the exercise in two days.

Do you see new things?

And then come back again after a week.

Do you now "suddenly" see other things, new directions?

Is there a connection between the new "discoveries" and your mood? The place you are in emotionally when looking at the drawing?

Does this influence interfere with the interpretation activity?

What do you think?

How can we avoid this?

Well, this is one of the important lessons on the way to becoming a sensitive and professional drawing interpreter. As I have recommended throughout the book, stay emotional; use that sensitivity to reach the child's emotional depths, to connect to their messages; stick to the facts you discover in the drawings; link them with the additional information that comes from other sources (parents, family, social workers, welfare professionals, the education system), in order to reinforce one direction or another. But in my view, *use the additional information only after you have a certain line of thought from the drawings you have seen, in order to reinforce it and not be influenced by it.*

FINAL CHAPTER - A PERSONAL AND PROFESSIONAL ENDING TO AN EMOTIONAL JOURNEY

Perspectives from the therapeutic field, final thoughts, words from the heart.

> **"The drawing is not an end, it is a beginning. A beginning of conversation, of understanding, of change."**

THE CORE TOOLS FOR WORKING WITH DRAWINGS

Introduction: The Importance of Working with Drawings

Throughout this book, we explored many ways in which drawings can be viewed as a window into the worlds of children, adolescents, and the family as a whole. Interpreting drawings is a highly valuable and effective tool that enables deep, professional observation of what is happening in the child's inner world and within family dynamics.

The Contribution of Interpretation to Parents and the Family

For parents, interpreting drawings serves as an everyday tool that allows them to see, feel, and understand the child's inner world. Beyond that, it opens a door to understanding relationships within the family and helps identify emotional processes and mutual influences among family members.

The Need for Broader Professional Recognition

Despite its importance, interpreting drawings is still not sufficiently recognized and appreciated among various professionals. We need to expand recognition and appreciation of this tool so that more therapists, educators, and parents can derive meaningful benefit from it in their work and daily life.

Summary of the Main Points Learned

I hope and believe that this book will help change the approach to interpreting children's and adolescents' drawings and will bring broad exposure to the subject in every home and around the world. To conclude, we will briefly revisit the central ideas learned in the book, which highlight the value and contribution of interpretation for all involved.

THE CORE TOOLS IN INTERPRETING DRAWINGS

Interpreting drawings rests on several core tools that allow deep, professional engagement with the child's emotional world. First and foremost is symbolic reading, understanding the symbolic meaning behind the elements that appear in the drawing. Alongside this, attention should be paid to colors, lines, placement, and the way they are expressed. Every detail in a drawing may reflect a particular emotional state, which can be assessed by considering proportions, composition, and the presence or absence of figures and elements. Beyond looking, it is recommended to open a conversation with the child and use the principles of curiosity, listening, and presence, tools that deepen understanding and give the child a sense of safety.

THE IMPACT OF INTERPRETATION ON EMOTIONAL, EDUCATIONAL, AND INTERPERSONAL PROCESSES

Interpreting a drawing is not meant to diagnose a specific problem, but to expand the toolbox for a deep understanding of the child. It enables us to notice hidden feelings such as fears, loneliness, joy, or hope, and to identify relationships, both within the family and with friends and adults.

In addition, it is possible to recognize patterns of behavior such as avoidance, control, people-pleasing, or outbursts. Interpreting drawings opens a door to understanding the child's self-perception by looking at figures, colors, lines, and even moments of silence in the drawing. It is important to emphasize that an accurate or "beautiful" drawing is not the goal; what matters is the ability to connect to the child who drew it and understand the message they wish to convey.

INTEGRATION WITH ADDITIONAL DIAGNOSTIC AND THERAPEUTIC TOOLS

Interpreting drawings does not stand alone; it integrates with other tools in assessment and treatment. It serves as another link in the chain of understanding the child, together with conversation, play, observations, and input from the immediate environment. Cooperation with teachers, therapists, doctors, and social workers is vital for achieving a broad and deep picture of the child's condition.

PROFESSIONAL RECOMMENDATIONS FOR THE ROAD AHEAD

This book is another step on the path to protecting children, adolescents, and the family, and is based on over twenty years of experience. It offers a range of perspectives and examples that enable anyone to become a better drawing interpreter. However, to reach high professional standards, persistence in the following is required: ongoing practice, staying up to date, learning, reading, and professional development. In addition, one must adhere to uncompromising professional ethics, a basic principle for anyone seeking to be a high-quality, humane, and dedicated professional.

SOMETHING FROM THE HEART: A PERSONAL STORY AND A CALLING

Coping with Childhood Trauma

In this book, I chose to share my personal story, a sexual assault I experienced at age ten, at school, by an older student. In those days, I had no one who would listen: not at school, and not at home, where we were all struggling with the hardships of survival stemming from my father's disability. And so, I found myself, a ten-year-old boy, standing alone before a deep abyss, with no hand outstretched to help, not even a hand to hold me so I would stop sinking into the depths.

The Effects of the Trauma

One of the clearest memories that remained with me concerns the fears that arose after the incident: fear of enclosed spaces, situations of having my hands tied, and of the police, arrest, and prison. The feelings of fear and dread accompanied me for years and were a direct outcome of that traumatic experience.

The Calling Born of Pain

Out of my personal pain and struggle, I found my way to the world of interpreting drawings by children, adolescents, and families. This calling became a way of life for me, a mission that saves souls, especially those who do not have the ability to cry out for help. When you act from a sense of calling, you understand that the road never ends: it is accompanied by constant seeking, learning, renewal, and an endless exposure to realizing the calling.

Understanding and Choosing the Profession

For many years, I knew that my true desire was to work with children and adolescents, yet the course of my life led me elsewhere. Only when a deep inner understanding arrived did I dare to take the first step on the path to my calling.

A PERSONAL TIP: COMBINING PROFESSIONALISM WITH EMOTION

What helped me move from being a professional to an outstanding one, both competent and humane, was the courage to rely not only on knowledge and professional tools, but also on the feelings of the heart and my personal intuition.

Do not be afraid to bring intuition and emotion into the process of interpreting drawings. Although at times they can mislead or prompt judgment, in my view, these are precisely the tools that allow us to be sharper, more attuned to the other's needs, and to act from the genuine professional ethics to which we are all committed.

Interpreting drawings naturally engages emotions, worries, fears, abilities, and functioning, all of which are suffused with emotion. Therefore, the more sensitively we use our emotions, the better and more accurate drawing interpreters we will succeed in being.

I believe that the true way to help children, adolescents, and families begins with truly seeing and listening to the other. When we really see the other, we can bring about change.

I invite you to keep asking, sharing, and developing. This knowledge belongs to all of us, and together we will create a more sensitive, perceptive, and caring world.

With love and appreciation,

Koby Avraham (M.A.)
Expert in interpreting drawings by children, adolescents, and families
"Seeing and Feeling Beyond Colors"

INTERPRETATION OF THE DRAWINGS IN THE PRACTICE CHAPTER

DRAWING NO. 1: THE HOUSE AND THE OPEN DOOR

Initial impression – pastoral, calm, and quiet.

Notable signs – the tree is slightly hidden by the house; the sense is that the tree is leaning on the house; the tree on the right side symbolizes the father, perhaps the father's longing for the members of the household, or theirs for the father.

The door is wide open to receive guests, welcoming and inviting one to enter the home. In other situations and contexts, the message might be the opposite: "come, hurry to see what is inside the house," but then the appearance of the house would likely be less safe and serene. Perhaps cracks in the walls, perhaps a crooked, broken roof, perhaps thick smoke from the chimney.

The path expresses a desire for change, to set out on a new path.

Note the house door: if you look closely, you can see that it is made of two parts; perhaps a disagreement about opening the door, perhaps a wish to open the door in stages, part by part.

The structure of the roof teaches us about a safe place inside the home; the person who drew it has a sense of stability and security; everything is in straight, steady lines. In terms of motor skills, the person who drew it shows stability of movement. At the same time, all the very straight lines may also indicate an obsession with order and cleanliness.

The light blue seen inside the house and through the windows hints at good verbal ability, confidence in the space, and environment.

The chimney is indeed without smoke, yet it seems to have a cover on it, as indicated by the small handle on it. Nevertheless, in light of the wide-open door, it seems there is no difficulty or need to transmit any messages, certainly not under coercion.

The tree trunk is wide at its base and becomes narrower, indicating "feet on the ground", yet the treetop branches look like two hands raised in possible surrender. The feeling I get from the tree is of physical or emotional distance from the father, who may not be around. Perhaps he left home; perhaps he works outside the home. In any case, based on the tree leaning on the house as if in a hugging posture, it seems there is longing, a lack. If the tree were meant to guard the house or its occupants, it would be much taller, with a thicker, stronger trunk, perhaps even with added roots.

This was the first interpretation of the sample drawing. I used, of course, my many years of experience, but also intuition, linking of messages and symbols, and the ability to "create" a story.

- So, how close were you in your interpretation?
- Who among you noticed that the door is divided into two?
- Who among you noticed the cap on the chimney?
- Who among you addressed the meaning of the color blue?

If you were close, wonderful; if not, that's excellent too, maybe you are heading in another new direction. At the same time, try to stay within the conventions and the international language of drawings.

So, one drawing, one interpretation; I will return to it again tomorrow, for my own practice.

DRAWING NO. 2: PLAYING IN THE PARK

My initial feeling from the drawing is power, ostracism, and a fight.

In the drawing, there are five children and one more figure, very far away on the horizon, in green. It seems the green figure is holding something in its hand.

In terms of my interpretation process, I divide the drawing into three areas and will try to find the connection from one area to another. To see whether the message fits together.

- The first area – the group of children at the front of the drawing.
- The second area – the distant child near the tree.
- The third area – the area of the green figure.

In the front area, we will look at the group of children who are chasing the ball. Already at first glance, one can see the hierarchy in the group. Who is the leader? Who do you think it is?

The girl in the striped shirt also appears physically the largest among the four. She is also closest to the ball. But note that her hands are folded, as if saying, "I am not going to bend down to pick up the ball." The other two children seem to be running in order to please her and pick up the ball. The last child in the group is a bit at a distance; this child is also physically the smallest. It seems the child is satisfied with their status with the group of children, "to be with the big kids."

As noted, the division of roles in this group is clear.

The second area is the child and the tree. From a distance, the child can convey several messages: first, I am envious; they are having fun together. On the other hand, the child might be ostracized by the other children. Another option is that perhaps the child is afraid of the children to such a degree that the child even moves away from them as much as possible.

The tree looks very much "like the child": bent, sad, without leaves. The tree looks almost dead. This gives a feeling of a real barrier between the child and the group of children at the front. If the tree is a person, perhaps the adult who is supposed to watch over the child, then that could certainly explain the great distance from the group: "There is no one to protect me; there is no one to hide behind."

Now, let us look at what appears on the horizon as a green figure. Are those the tree's leaves? Is there a connection to the protection the child needs? Perhaps. What is the role of the green figure according to your sense? It seems to be the voice of the one who drew, the voice within the subconscious.

- Who do you think drew the drawing, anyway?
- One of the children in the front group?
- Maybe the child by the tree?

- Or maybe it's actually the green man?

Note: I keep repeating the word maybe, putting on the page all the options I see. Especially at the beginning, this is an important process: to raise all the options, for every drawing, all the time. Ultimately, we need to try to connect the messages to "the child's story." In the next stage, we will receive information from the parents and the professionals, cross-check what we see in the drawing with the child's situation and with the documentation, and then arrive at the optimal understanding of the real story. We will be able to offer our solutions to the difficulty and provide the most suitable tools, as close as possible to the reality of the child's life.

DRAWING NO. 3: THE ADULT, THE CHILD, AND THE THREAD

My initial impression of the drawing: a grandfather going for a walk with his grandson. It looks calm; both are neatly dressed, in a pleasant, smiling atmosphere. Sometimes that is actually a sign of the opposite, a deliberate misdirection. "I draw a positive appearance, but the message is actually the opposite." These cases typically recur when there is fear and anxiety toward close relatives. And when I "look deeper," a number of things catch my attention.

- The first is, of course, the rope that connects the adult to the child.
- Second, it seems the child is wearing two pairs of pants, long and short.
- The adult's small ears compared with the proportions of his body, especially if they are almost the size of the child's ear.
- The adult's groin area is accentuated.
- The child's gaze looks frightened, directed toward the floor and not toward the adult.

Interpretation

This strange rope or thread immediately draws the eye. If you enlarge the image (by the way, I always recommend doing this in the interpretation process), you will see that the adult is not actually holding the rope; it is attached to the joint of the index finger. The rope reaches the child's arm. Notice what happens? It looks as though the rope is around the muscle, but it also looks as though the thread is unraveling from the shirt, as if the adult pulled the thread, whether by accident or not.

This raises questions. If, for example, it were a grandfather going for a walk with his grandson, then if there were a rope, it would presumably be attached to a harness in an orderly way, as is customary in several places around the world. And the "grandfather" would be holding the strap in his hand for the grandson's safety.

But in my view, that is not what is happening. The child's downward gaze, with eyes that convey pressure, not toward the "grandfather," and the lack of holding the rope or the thread unraveling from the shirt, all add up to a sense that this is a coercive situation.

Another thing that strengthens this feeling is the adult's groin area: it is very emphasized, with an accentuating addition in something that looks like half a belt, toward the child, so that he will see it.

True, in jeans that's the design, but not this conspicuously.

Another point: the adult's ears, relative to the adult's size and physique, are very small, especially if we look at the child's ears; there is almost no difference between them. This adds the element of not listening, or an unwillingness to listen, perhaps to what the child "is saying."

Another thing is what appears under the adult's eyes. True, it's not unusual, but it is not expected given the adult's youthful, well-built body.

Recommendations

In this case, I would ask to check whether additional signs of coercion by an adult appear, or any coercion at all. Therefore, I would ask for a drawing of a family, of a playground, and also a drawing of the kindergarten or the school.

If talking with the child about the drawing, I would ask the child, "Where are you and Grandpa going for a walk?" Based on the answer, we can steer the conversation. "That's not Grandpa" would be an answer that strengthens this direction, and we should continue the conversation with care and consideration.

DRAWING NO. 4: THE PARENTS, THE JUDGING GIRL

The initial feeling about the drawing is quite clear: an argument between parents, with the girl in the center between them, trying to separate them, is it indeed the case?

My interpretive sequence will be to raise questions for reflection, and afterward, I will address each person in the situation separately and then integrate them.

- Is this a family?
- Is this the family's composition?
- Are figures missing from the family? Who, and why?
- Who is more aggressive in the argument? Based on what?
- Which side does the girl choose? Based on what?
- What is the meaning of the difference in the shape of the mother's and the father's eyes?

Interpretation

Let's analyze the figures separately and then unify the information into one broader picture. When we examine the mother, we notice that she is frightened or defensive. How? What are the signs of this?

The hands are close to the chest in a protective pose, with clenched fists. Both of the mother's legs are together and closed in a steady stance. It looks as if the mother, body straight, is defending herself and standing guard.

In contrast, the father appears to be moving toward the mother, striding, with the upper half of his body leaning forward toward her, including his arms. Unlike the mother, the palms are open. As an initial impression, together with the body movement, there is a sense that a "slap in the face" is on its way from the father. But could it be that a different intention is involved?

A clenched fist is a basic state of defense or attack, a physical readiness in the face of threat, or the exertion of force. It is a classic muscular state of anger. In quite a few cases, it is a sign of a person holding themselves back to prevent an outburst, a kind of self-control. Another possibility is fear and anxiety; the body feels threatened and naturally responds by locking the fists in readiness for defense.

If we look at it from a relationship's perspective, the fist can serve as a marker for setting a physical boundary, that is: "Stay away from me, or I will attack you."

An open palm is an inviting element, receptive, open to dialogue, extended for giving and cooperation, from a person who is usually quiet and calm.

So, what is actually happening here?

The one who shed light on the situation is the daughter in the middle. You can see that the girl is in an attacking body posture toward the father, standing guard, facing him, a hand with a fist raised forward toward the father, while her gaze is directed at his legs to keep track of the steps of the "violent" father.

As a starting point, we assumed this is a family. If that is not the case and it is a threatening stranger, the emotional domain may change, but the body posture remains interpreted the same way, because the bodily signs and their messages stay as they were.

DRAWING NO. 5: LOVE WITH A STAIN ON THE FOREHEAD

Initial impression: It seems to be social ostracism; the boy looks sad, while all the children around him are smiling. Let's investigate.

Interpretation

This time in our interpretation, we will examine the drawing in two aspects: the placement of the figures and an analysis of the figure. We can see that the boy is at the center of the picture, significantly larger than the other children in the drawing, so large that he occupies space from bottom to top. This teaches us, without a doubt, that he is the center of the story. On both sides of him are two groups of children, three and two. They are all small yet smiling, standing at the bottom of the page. The group on the right is on the social side, and the group on the left is on the family side.

As noted, the very fact that he is large tells us he is the center of the story. His hands are close to his body, giving the sense that they are clasped behind his back, perhaps as a sign of his sadness. The neck is very thin and small compared with his enormous head, indicating some emotional difficulty and a lack of ability to express himself. The head is located in the upper two-thirds of the page, which is where the areas of ego, spirit, emotion, dreams, and fantasies lie.

In my opinion, the boy's enormous size and his central placement completely rule out the possibility of social ostracism. If it were social ostracism, the boy would likely be very small, probably in a corner of the page; the children would be in one group; they certainly would not all be looking at him, and would probably be turning their backs on him and not physically close to him.

Let's examine the face: the boy's mouth is curved in a way that indicates sadness; the left side of the mouth curves more to the left, which hints at warmth and love. Note the triangular nose!

The triangle shape in children's drawings: A triangle is a form that suggests two main themes. The first is criticalness: the apex of the triangle indicates toward whom the criticism is directed, and the width of the base indicates the degree or intensity of the criticism. The second domain, as noted, is sexuality and what is connected to it, for better and for worse.

Let's look at the nose: the apex is oriented toward the head, which indicates the child's self-criticism in the realm of thoughts and cognitive processing; the width of the base shows that the criticism is not minor.

Let's move up toward the forehead, where we notice a red stain; if we enlarge the photo (remember, I always recommend enlarging), we will see it is in the shape of a broken heart, interesting. Let's return for a moment to the nose triangle; the apex is directed toward the broken heart. Moving on to the eyes: they are very large and glance toward the group of girls on the right. There, we can see that the girl in green has only one arm, which may hint at an inability to hug, which may connect her to the story.

Unlike the initial sense of social ostracism, as we progressed in analyzing the drawing, the signs pointed more and more toward unrequited love; perhaps an inability to correctly translate physical signs and messages into emotional signals. The children's gazes toward the older boy give me a sense of admiration, and it is possible that this is a boy who is the "king of the class."

So, from social ostracism to unrequited love, this shows how alert we must be to the drawing and to the signs. As the saying goes, we must read the "fine print."

DRAWING NO. 6: THE ENTRANCE TO DARKNESS

Initial impression, hesitation before an important decision by the child or the adolescent.

This is a special drawing, with very few details to help us approach the interpretation of the drawing. All in all, three or four central objects. Let's think about a strategy for interpretation.

For that reason, I think we should focus on the colors in the drawing, as well as on the square elements in the background of the child or the adolescent.

The first frame is gray, confusion, emotional detachment, difficulty in expressing emotions, energy, and a feeling of fatigue.

The second frame is blue, calm, tranquility, a need for security, closeness, and personal safety; when the blue is dark, there is also a possibility of a depressive tendency and withdrawal.

Finally, the black part may hint at emotional overload, fear, sadness, depression, repressed anger, and a need for control.

The boy's shirt, a combination of yellow and green: optimism, joy, a need for attention, a sociable child, curiosity, high energy, and also a need for structure.

It is important to note that a shirt is a personal garment, close to the heart and the head; it represents the inner self.

The Story of the Drawing

The feeling in the drawing is that the adolescent is just beforc entering what appears to be a dark room, with the blue frame giving the impression of the doorframe.

The colors of the shirt tell us that the adolescent is optimistic and has a zest for life; therefore, it seems he is in a stage of withdrawal. The look in the eyes is sad; they seem to be asking for help, looking for someone to advise them on what to do.

In conclusion, after the interpretation, it seems to me that my initial intuition is close to the drawing's true story.

DRAWINGS NO. 7 AND 8: – THE BIRDS ON THE TREE

Here, for the first time, we will practice interpreting two drawings that are very similar; yet as we move further and further into the stages of interpretation, we understand that there are different messages in each of the drawings. To make comprehension and reading easier, we will do this with the help of a table.

What We're Looking At	Drawing 7	Drawing 8
Two drawings that look exactly the same, are they really?		
Elements in the Drawing	A drawing in a variety of magnificent colors that gives a sense of nature, pastoralism, and optimism. A house with many windows,	Here too, a drawing in a variety of magnificent colors, which gives a pleasant feeling of life in

What We're Looking At	Drawing 7	Drawing 8
Two drawings that look exactly the same, are they really?		
	a path to the house, a water lake, a tree with leaves and fruits, a bird, blue skies, and clouds. A mountain range in the background.	nature. A house with a path leading to it, a large door without windows but with a chimney, a bench near the house, a tree with fruits, some of which are on the ground, without leaves, blue skies with clouds, and a mountain range

What We're Looking At	Drawing 7	Drawing 8
Two drawings that look exactly the same, are they really?		
		in the background.
Initial Feeling	Freedom, hope, optimism, anticipation for the future, a good life.	Something in this drawing is more limited, feels more cramped, less space, more fixation to the ground. Routine, concealment.

What We're Looking At	Drawing 7	Drawing 8
Two drawings that look exactly the same, are they really?		
The House	Based on the path's appearance, the house is located in a low place. The house is well-built, straight, balanced, and level. It has large windows, all with bars. Two facts raise questions, especially concerning the drawing's pastoral appearance: first, there is no visible entrance door – does a door even exist? The windows are barred, and the	Based on the path, this house is in a high place, perhaps difficult to reach. The door is very large, almost half the height of the house. It seems as if the house's colors have 'swapped'—the walls are red, and the roof is black. The house has no windows at all,

What We're Looking At	Drawing 7	Drawing 8
Two drawings that look exactly the same, are they really?		
	interior of the house seen through them is black, although the window on the far left side is bright.	except for two small, high circles that could be windows or lanterns. The house has a chimney, but no smoke, no message coming out of the house, no windows, and a closed door, so we essentially have no way of seeing what is happening

What We're Looking At	Drawing 7	Drawing 8
Two drawings that look exactly the same, are they really?		
		inside the house from the outside. If we look closely, the facade of the house can be likened to a shouting, angry face, with squeezed eyes (the lanterns) and a very large mouth (the door).

What We're Looking At	Drawing 7	Drawing 8
Two drawings that look exactly the same, are they really?		
The Tree	The tree is very central, high, magnificent in its beauty, tall, and towering, with a high, upright treetop, branches, leaves, and fruits in a variety of colors. The spread of the branches suggests an intellectual person with developed analytical and artistic abilities, capable of taking a process from start to finish and reaping the fruits.	Despite this tree's size, like in Drawing 7, it is very significant to the story of the drawing. However, there are several very significant differences. The tree here is on the side of the drawing, the side of the family and the mother, which has significance

What We're Looking At	Drawing 7	Drawing 8
Two drawings that look exactly the same, are they really?		
	The variety of colors suggests the range of possibilities they can manage and succeed in. The tree is far from the house and appears to be overlooking the house from the top of the hill, looking down; from there, it also looks towards the horizon beyond the sea. An orange bird sits on the treetop, also looking toward the house. However,	either as the mother's protection or a blockage, depending on the additional details in the drawing. We also notice fruits in the treetop, but without leaves. The fruits are one color, representing one path of capability.

What We're Looking At	Drawing 7	Drawing 8
Two drawings that look exactly the same, are they really?		
	it seems the tree itself blocks the possibilities for development overseas; its entire treetop 'sits' and blocks the sea passage between the ranges.	There are also fruits on the ground here, which may indicate that no one has come to pick the fruits for a long time or that it hasn't been watered, and the fruits are falling. The bird sitting on the tree is in two colors—blue and red, the colors of the house—it sits

What We're Looking At	Drawing 7	Drawing 8
Two drawings that look exactly the same, are they really?		
		on a broken branch, as if overlooking the house and acting as a 'complementary color' to the house; it has a direct link to what is happening inside the house.

What We're Looking At	Drawing 7	Drawing 8
Two drawings that look exactly the same, are they really?		
The Path	The path to the house gives a feeling of descent. The color and shade are pleasant; it is also clear of obstacles, and its end seems to lead to the hidden door of the house. Overall, the path reflects the general positive atmosphere of the entire drawing.	The path in this drawing is shiny, slippery, with a sharp angle in the direction of the ascent to the house. The feeling is one of effort to climb it to get home. It certainly fits well with the mystery of the house and what is happening inside it.

What We're Looking At	Drawing 7	Drawing 8
Two drawings that look exactly the same, are they really?		
The Mountain Range	The mountain range in this drawing is lower, with more moderate slopes, making it easier to move on them. In Drawing 7, they are essentially ridges on both sides of the lake, suggesting there is a passage and movement through them, even though the tree blocks the view. A sense of freedom of movement on and	In Drawing 8, the mountain range is shorter, likely due to the proximity to the drawer. Here, too, there is a possibility for passage and movement, but the feeling is that everything is close and cramped. What is different and significant here is the

What We're Looking At	Drawing 7	Drawing 8
Two drawings that look exactly the same, are they really?		
	from the mountains is still conveyed; they are distant and blend into the landscape as a pastoral scene.	topographical structure of the mountains; they look more like sharp pyramids, the sides of the mountains at sharper angles, giving a feeling of difficulty and pressure. Also, we mentioned that a triangle is a critical feature in drawings; this also seems to align with the

What We're Looking At	Drawing 7	Drawing 8
Two drawings that look exactly the same, are they really?		
		mystery of the house.
Summary	A pastoral, pleasant, and optimistic drawing, matching the initial feeling. It seems there is a potential for success overseas, or at least such aspirations with a high chance of success. Despite this, there are hesitations, conflicts about whether to embark	Drawing 8, although it looks pleasant with nice colors, as we examine the signs, we get the feeling of restriction, mysterious information inside the house with no possibility of

What We're Looking At	Drawing 7	Drawing 8
Two drawings that look exactly the same, are they really?		
	on the journey or not. There is definitely a point of light on the left side of the house. The bird sitting on the treetop also hints at the desire and aspiration to fly far away, but it is also frozen, not flying, waiting for the right moment to set out.	knowing through clues. It does not seem that the matters mentioned are related to violence or an extreme situation. The person inside the house feels stable and strong but is still concealing. The bird sits on a broken branch, with the house's

What We're Looking At	Drawing 7	Drawing 8
Two drawings that look exactly the same, are they really?		
		colors, which, as stated, indicate a connection to the house and what is happening there. The broken branch suggests some kind of break, a setback, at a certain point in time. The bird sitting on the broken branch is either trying to hide this break

What We're Looking At	Drawing 7	Drawing 8
Two drawings that look exactly the same, are they really?		
		or is waiting to exploit this break for change, to fly to a new place, but it is still waiting. The drawer is still waiting for the right moment.

DRAWING NO. 11: A WARM SUN, OR A COLD ONE?

Initial impression: a head-on confrontation between a child or adolescent and his mother. Apparently, on a matter fundamental to both the mother and her son.

Let us begin by dividing the drawing into visual elements.

We have, all told, three main elements: the sun, the mountains, and the boy/adolescent.

Let us start with the adolescent. His posture looks strong and confident, even proud. Note the angle of the head, perhaps even arrogance, or disregard for the sun, the mother. Although it looks as if he is looking toward her, actually, he is not, and this amplifies the sense of pride and disregard. His eyes are practically closed; again, this can suggest ignoring, or in response to "the heat" of the sun.

The sun, as we have learned, the sun is a reflection of the relationship between the mother and the drawer, as the drawer experiences it. This sun is very interesting: it is enormous, taking over more than two-thirds of the drawing page. That means it is likewise dominant in the drawer's life; significantly controlling the time in the child's life, whether through influence or in practical time.

The body of the sun is composed of three rings in different shades of yellow, which can tell us about instability in the intensity of the warmth and love that the drawer feels coming from the mother. Perhaps he feels a ring that is choking him, the one at the center of the sun.

Pay attention to something special. Take a look at the sun's rays; we actually see two systems of sun rays here. The yellow ones, and if we step back a little from the image, we can also distinguish an additional system of thick, orange sun rays. For a moment, this looked like a large sunflower. However, when we see the mountains in the middle, in a brownish-gray color, completely devoid of vegetation and life, more reminiscent of the soil of Mars, we realize that this sun is very hot. It is so large and hot that it burns every good patch of land over large areas.

The relationship between the child and the mother is difficult, threatening, and rigid, a continuous rigidity. In fact, even if the child tries to get close to the sun, to the mother, he will be badly burned. A very interesting and extreme drawing in its portrayal of a mother–son relationship.

DRAWINGS NO. 13 AND 14: THE MAN AND THE KNIFE 1 AND 2

We will conduct a comparison between two drawings that are very similar in terms of the situation. Are they also different in terms of each one's content and message? We will examine the two drawings step by step. We will do this in a table so we can see the parallels between the drawings and the differences between them.

What We Examine	**Drawing 13**	**Drawing 14**
Pay attention to how similar the two drawings are. Look at the drawings, at the smallest details. Try to learn about the difference between them—is there a difference at all? Let's begin.		
Initial Feeling	The figure looks cunning, the type that tries to	A figure that looks aggressive and threatening,

What We Examine	Drawing 13	Drawing 14
Pay attention to how similar the two drawings are. Look at the drawings, at the smallest details. Try to learn about the difference between them—is there a difference at all? Let's begin.		
	persuade; something between a salesperson and a swindler.	suggesting even physical harm. A situation of physical threat, perhaps also defensive.
The Background	Blue skies with added clouds create a	The background of the two shades—green and

What We Examine	Drawing 13	Drawing 14
Pay attention to how similar the two drawings are. Look at the drawings, at the smallest details. Try to learn about the difference between them—is there a difference at all? Let's begin.		
	pleasant, somewhat pastoral atmosphere. The man with the knife is in an open space, which may teach us that this is a less physically violent situation	brown—gives me a more focused atmosphere on the man and the knife, less on the background and the surrounding atmosphere. The colors brown and green are colors of

What We Examine	Drawing 13	Drawing 14
Pay attention to how similar the two drawings are. Look at the drawings, at the smallest details. Try to learn about the difference between them—is there a difference at all? Let's begin.		
	and hints more at something possibly related to persuasion.	stability and growth.
Eye Gaze	The direction of the eyes gaze seems general, toward the audience or the	A gaze focused on the knives blade, giving the feeling that the figure is conveying the

What We Examine	Drawing 13	Drawing 14
Pay attention to how similar the two drawings are. Look at the drawings, at the smallest details. Try to learn about the difference between them—is there a difference at all? Let's begin.		
	people the figure is talking to; they are the target or the center and focus of the conversation.	message to the person opposite them through the knife, as if saying to the knife: If they don't behave, I will use you.
The Knife's Shape	The knife is large and wide,	The knife is very long; it can harm a

What We Examine	Drawing 13	Drawing 14
Pay attention to how similar the two drawings are. Look at the drawings, at the smallest details. Try to learn about the difference between them—is there a difference at all? Let's begin.		
	but it has a short handle. A short handle provides no leverage/power, so its use is gentler and easier—cutting vegetables, perhaps fish, or meat into small	physically more distant person. The handle is also very long, serving as a leverage point for strength and power. The sharp, long blade allows the person holding the knife to stab it into a

What We Examine	Drawing 13	Drawing 14
Pay attention to how similar the two drawings are. Look at the drawings, at the smallest details. Try to learn about the difference between them—is there a difference at all? Let's begin.		
	pieces. A less threatening knife.	wider body or even have the knife emerge from the other side.
The Knife Grip	The grip of the knife in this drawing is almost unseen, giving a feeling	In this drawing, the entire gripping hand is visible; it looks stronger and more muscular.

What We Examine	Drawing 13	Drawing 14
Pay attention to how similar the two drawings are. Look at the drawings, at the smallest details. Try to learn about the difference between them—is there a difference at all? Let's begin.		
	of a light hold, a grip without force, not one intended to cause harm.	The grip on the knife's butt is also strong, one where a lot of force is applied so that it won't drop, or so that the stab will be stronger.

What We Examine	Drawing 13	Drawing 14
Pay attention to how similar the two drawings are. Look at the drawings, at the smallest details. Try to learn about the difference between them—is there a difference at all? Let's begin.		
Facial Expression	The face conveys disloyalty or cunning, brewing schemes, but I don't get a sense of malice/evil.	I sense malice and cruelty from the facial expression; all the facial muscles convey a feeling of tension—a difficult person.

What We Examine	Drawing 13	Drawing 14
Pay attention to how similar the two drawings are. Look at the drawings, at the smallest details. Try to learn about the difference between them—is there a difference at all? Let's begin.		
In Conclusion	One is cunning, a manipulator.	One that conveys malice/evil for me. In any case, these feelings need reinforcement and support from additional drawings or information from another source.

DRAWING NO. 15: MOTHER? GIRL?

Initial impression: A very young girl in advanced pregnancy.

In analyzing this drawing, we will draw on material that addresses the sun as representing the relationship between the mother and the person who drew the picture. We will examine how this is expressed. First, we begin with a graphic description of the image: a very young woman, appearing to be a teenage girl, heavily pregnant. She holds in her hand a baby or a doll. The sun (the young woman's mother) is positioned at the top left, in the family area. The young woman's back is turned toward the sun. The atmosphere in the drawing is very calm, with light blue clouds in a tranquil mood.

Let us now delve into the depths of the drawing. The girl or very young adolescent is in an advanced pregnancy, holding a baby or a doll in her hand. But note: the girl is not holding the baby; she is not even in contact with him. The baby reaches a hand toward the young woman. Another very interesting point is that the baby has half a body, only the upper torso. Perhaps this is a baby who has not yet completed the birth process and has not yet come into the world? He is not yet part of the young woman's lived reality. Therefore, she is also not holding or supporting the baby, as if we are halfway through the process.

The light blue clouds surround the young girl, as if she is floating, and she, too, is shown only in the upper half of her body, just like the baby, still in the midst of the process.

And what is happening to the sun? The sun's face looks very surprised as she looks at the young woman and the baby. The sun's rays teach us about the mother's ongoing criticism of the young girl (her daughter). According to the rays, there is also an emotional distance between the mother and her daughter. This is an interesting situation in their relationship.

If we weave everything into a single story, it seems we are looking at a young woman who conceived at a very young age. She is in the midst of emotionally and mentally processing the pregnancy and what still lies ahead. It seems she is not yet fully prepared for it, yet according to her calm and smiling face, she is self-assured about the future. The person who is not happy about this is the young woman's mother, who criticizes her for the situation, but the young woman is self-confident. She turns her back to the mother, as if ignoring her criticism.

DRAWING NO. 16: FAMILY ON THE MOVE

The family is a school for life; family drawings are a treasure in the hands of those who interpret drawings. One can obtain information about almost any area related to the child's life. And as I keep saying throughout the book, it all begins and ends with the family.

My initial feeling from the drawing: the family is hurrying to get to a family event; they are running late.

The family is dressed well. From the careful clothing, we can infer that the family's economic situation is good, perhaps above average. The family has five members: a couple and three children, two girls and a boy.

The family looks close; they are walking side by side and holding hands, except for the girl in purple. She is also a step or two away from the family line, and she is not holding the father's hand (here we can ask, why?). The color of the dress, burgundy-purple, what does this color tell us in the color table? Will the qualities of this color fit the overall story?

The one at the center of attention is the young boy in the middle; both parents are holding his hands. The father goes further and looks straight at him. Perhaps worried? Perhaps angry? Perhaps urging him on?

Who, in your view, is the dominant figure in the family?

In my view, the mother is without doubt the dominant figure, the one who makes the decisions and leads the family forward. It is quite possible that, from additional drawings or information we receive, we will learn that the mother is a figure who is outside the home, perhaps the breadwinner.

The father appears more family-oriented. Note: Remember the chapter on the placement of elements on the drawing page. We learned that the "normal" placement in the family is the father on the right and the mother on the left. Here it is reversed: the mother is on the right (what is done outside the home) and the father on the left (the domestic). This is important information about a "role reversal."

The girl is behind; this can also indicate the distance she feels from the family or from the family unit. The father's "lack of interest" may indicate emotional distance from the girl; alternatively, the father trusts the girl and therefore allows her to be behind. How does it look to you?

Who do you think drew this drawing?

If it is the girl in purple, she has come to tell us she does not feel part of the family. Perhaps she is an adopted child? She feels that the whole family is walking forward and hurrying, without her. Perhaps she simply finds it hard to reach the family - a possible place for intervention.

Can we learn about the relationship between the father and the mother? How? What does this drawing teach us?

In any case, the family is very close; it seems there is only a need to bridge several areas in the communication among them all. The "Family Sits to Draw" model is a therapeutic model that would be very suitable here to get additional information and different perspectives on the relationships. A joint drawing session with the help of a facilitator can also greatly assist communication within the family.

Do you remember the sun in children's drawings? What does it mean? The sun appears in over 80% of children's drawings. Here it is missing. Does that connect with what we see in the family drawing?

Return to the drawing again and again; try to glean additional details. Perhaps another clue is hiding in the clothing?

DRAWING NO. 17: A TRIANGLE OF ANIMALS IN DIALOGUE

A drawing whose focus is animals; we will interpret the drawing through this theme. My initial impression is that this is a meeting of animals engaged in mediation; the dog is the mediator.

Interpretation

We will begin by learning the main characters, the dog, the raccoon, and the fox. Once we know them, we can personify and understand the human situation the child who drew it had in mind, and their message.

> Dog — loyalty, openness, and communication, as well as a need for protection and secure closeness.
> Fox — cunning, wisdom, and quick adaptation.
> Raccoon — alertness, a tendency to hide things or keep secrets.

The three animals stand in a circle, close together, looking at one another. There is mutual communication between the animals.

The faithful, loving yellow dog serves here as mediator and peacemaker; it is on the central axis, the subject of the drawing, the bearer of the message. Its face is pleasant and calm; it is relaxed, listening with great attentiveness to the other two animals. From the child's perspective, the dog can also represent a mediating authority, an educator such as a parent, a teacher, or a preschool teacher.

The other two animals are very different in character; each represents a different figure in the child's life. If we try to delve into the child's thinking, perhaps this is about disagreements between the parents or friends, with the child at the center, trying to mediate and bring the two closer. In fact, it could also be the child's inner thoughts, an internal conflict in which each animal represents a different opinion or idea.

In the chapter on animals, we mentioned that an animal in children's drawings can represent a good animal and a bad animal. What would happen to the interpretation if, in conversation with the child, they were to say that the dog is a good animal and the raccoon and the fox are bad animals? Broadly speaking, the interpretation would not change because of the fundamental traits of each animal.

Foxes are known as cunning animals, stealthy and deceptive. They likely represent a figure the child does not trust, with fear of a surprise at any given moment. A lack of security toward this person, a figure who feels dangerous and deceptive to the child.

The raccoon can tell us about a person who tends to hide things, steal, or act in secret; for the child, this signals unreliability, someone confusing who keeps their distance.

And it is reasonable to assume that the child is the dog, pleasant, nice, and secure, loving and loyal. It is possible that the child is seeking a safe and protective space for himself from the other two.

DRAWING NO. 19: THE SIBLINGS, AT HOME?

Initial impression – distress of two children, entering a house through the window, apparently not their family's home.

My interpretation of the drawing begins with the sad expression in the eyes of the two children; one is older than the other; there is no hint as to whether they are siblings or not. Their eyes are very sad, conveying sadness that is deep and prolonged, not something momentary. The child on the left, who seems younger, has his whole posture bent, conveying fatigue and exhaustion.

The children do not appear anxious, so we can assume they are not running away; it looks more as if they are seeking shelter. They also look neatly dressed and groomed, so they apparently are not lacking, but they project great sadness.

If I were to conduct an investigation into their situation through the drawing, I would ask them to draw their family. It is quite possible we would discover a lack or difficulty in one of the family members or one of the parents. Combining the information from the two drawings by the two siblings would allow us to understand what is happening in their lives. Of course, this is only a hypothesis. Let us return to the drawing itself. We will try to learn from it as many details as possible.

I open the interpretation table and begin to write down everything I see, and then try to understand the story behind this drawing alone.

The colors – somewhat pale, but there is a difference. The green and the sky blue that form the background of the drawing, where they are coming from suggests a more optimistic, lively, and growing place. In contrast, the color of the interior of the house, or the place they are entering, looks somewhat pale, a light brown.

Notice the younger child on the left, the one who looks sadder: he is wearing a gray shirt, and his hair is also gray. From what we know about the symbolism of gray, we understand there is a message of emotional detachment and an attempt to be 'unseen.' There is fatigue and exhaustion here.

The color of the child's shirt on the right is a brown tone, grounded, emotionally, and physically stable.

What is particularly interesting is the state of the window. Notice that the window frame is not connected at the bottom. Is this a message from the two that they lack a frame, or that there is a break in their framework, perhaps in their family unit?

Where are they trying to enter? Why through the window and not the door? Is this the house where they live?

Questions we cannot answer based on this drawing. Therefore, we will need more drawings to understand the story behind it.

The children's hands are in entirely different positions: the older child places both palms on the window, suggesting that he is active, taking action, whereas the other child's hands are not visible at all, which fits with his body curling inward and reinforces the sense of weakness and sadness.

DRAWING NO. 20: PRIDE TOWER

Initial impression from the drawing: an event related, by virtue of the colors, to the LGBTQ community.

We will divide the drawing according to the locations we learned in the chapter devoted to the placement of elements on the sheet of paper. We clearly see that the center of the drawing is the immense tower, which reaches the very top edge of the page and seems to sit on something that looks like a mountain peak; a path leads up to the tower's closed door. In addition, two pairs of trees are drawn, one pair on each side of the path, as well as one four-legged animal on each side of the path; the animals' color appears in the same shade as the lower part of the tower, where the large door is located. Approximately a third of the way up the tower, the colorful stripes that strongly recall the colors of the LGBTQ flag begin. At the top of the tower is a red triangular roof; the tower, in fact, looks like a rocket at liftoff, and also like a phallus. Reinforcing this impression are the clouds that look as if the rocket is cutting through them on its flight into the sky. On the tower are two windows, painted over the colors of the LGBTQ flag, closed. We can also see the animals, which look like donkeys, symbolizing the struggle and determination through hard work of the LGBTQ community.

On the face of it, it seems as if this is a poster or message from the LGBTQ community, a message from the LGBTQ community to the world.

What changes my mind, that we are not dealing here with a message from the community as a whole, are two things. The first is the fact that the tower's windows are closed and set into the tower wall; the second is the sun, located at the edge of the tower, red, angry, with no rays at all, which indicates a disconnect from the mother, or the mother's anger and disregard toward the person who drew it.

My interpretation is that this is a drawing made by a child or adolescent, boy or girl, who is "in the closet" and in the process of breaking out, coming out of the closet, toward freedom. And the mother is there, red with shame, ignoring the process even though she is so close to the top of the tower.

This small sun changes the whole picture, or, more precisely, our interpretation of the drawing. It teaches us that it is important to pay attention to every sign and element, even if it seems negligible and perhaps unimportant. In the case of a broader investigation, of course, we would need to examine the other drawings to see whether our interpretation is reinforced in them.

In conclusion, it seems that the initial feeling was correct regarding the general subject that concerns the LGBTQ community. But only after revisiting the image and attending to the additional details in it did we arrive at the possibility that this is a personal struggle related to "coming out of the closet."

DRAWING NO. 22: THE THREE CROSSES

Initial feeling: escape, fleeing from threatening difficulties, perhaps from things connected to religion.

Interpretation

The drawing in gray tones already leads us to feelings of gloom, darkness, and grayness that the person who drew it is experiencing. The sky and clouds are gray; the mountains in the background are very high, giving a sense of great difficulty in climbing them, and their shape is triangular.

Another prominent symbol is the cross. Three crosses appear in the drawing: two on the right that look like the crosses have undergone extreme hardship, and the third cross at the summit of the mountain appears large, stable, and fresh. The first two crosses are beyond the row of cypresses, whereas the third, strong cross is in line with the cypresses, completely exposed.

Crosses and intersections in children's and adolescents' drawings

As a reminder, in the first chapter, we discussed the stages of drawing development. In the advanced scribbling stage (ages 2-4), the cross appears for the first time. Here are several explanations regarding the cross.

Merging of different worlds — the horizontal line: material, everyday. The vertical line: spiritual, internal, and moral.

The meeting point — a significant point in the drawer's life, a crossroads, a decision point.

Conflict, collision — sometimes it refers to disagreements, a clash of opposing forces, internal and external. The location of the intersection and the size of the lines teach us about the level of tension and the balance between them.

Another element regarding the cross in Christianity is the phrase "In the name of the Father, the Son, and the Holy Spirit." We will return to this later in the analysis of the drawing.

Let us enter the depth of the drawing: the path begins on the right side, the social side, and reaches the left side, which connects to family and the past, to history. The figure walking on the path gives us the correct orientation, in this case, from right to left, from the social side to the family, the past. There seems to be a hint of returning home, to the family and the past. The child walking along the path looks exhausted, like one who has been through a difficult road.

The three crosses can provide us with further content. The right-hand cross is still in the shape of a cross; the second, the middle one, looks broken, as if the "arms" express despair; and the third cross is large, strong, and stable. If we return for a moment to the phrase "In the name of the Father, the Son, and the Holy Spirit," the right-hand cross is the Father, still standing upright yet looking somewhat tired, standing with its arms to the sides as if blocking the way or shielding so that one passes to its right, to the social area. The middle cross is "the Son," weak and broken, and it looks like a desperate person who has lost his way. The third cross, "the Holy Spirit," is strong, stable, steadfast, and resolute. The Son is between the Father and the Holy Spirit, who protect and watch over him on his way back home, to Christianity, to the Holy Spirit. Amazing!!!

DRAWING NO. 23: THE STORM FROM RIGHT AND LEFT

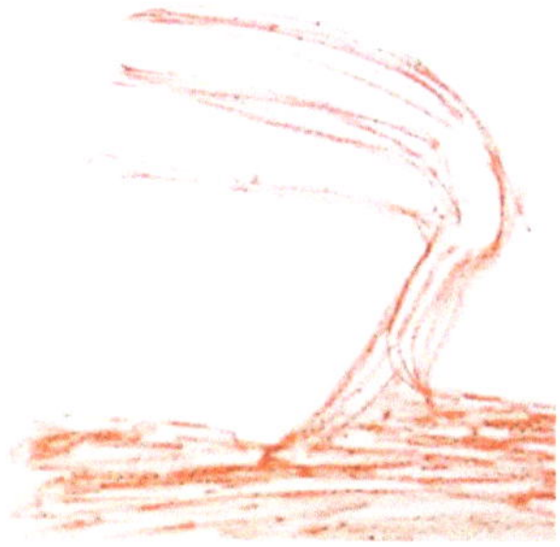

We dealt with the tree at length and devoted a special chapter to it. This time, I want to "use" the tree to discuss the regime of forces at work in the drawing.

My initial feeling is of a prolonged power struggle; you can see that the tree has survived harsh battles. It does not bud, does not blossom, does not grow, only survives.

First, let us address the tree's placement: it occupies 100% of the page. The tree, or what it represents, is the central subject of the drawing.

Its trunk is well-anchored in the ground; it begins in the center and extends toward the right.

I chose this specific drawing because it is clearly subjected to opposing forces. In the upper part of the branches and in the lower part of the trunk. Which forces? Who is applying the forces? Why are the forces opposed?

Let's try to locate the forces.

According to the shape of the trunk, we can see that forces are being applied to the trunk from left to right. Go back for a moment to the chapter on the page's spatial layout in interpreting children's drawings.

From the left come the mother, the family, warmth, the past, and the home. We will return to this.

The branches absorb pressure from right to left, and what is on the right?

On the right lies the social domain, everything outside the home: the father, renewal, development, work, learning, the need for change, the need to move forward.

So, what is really happening there?

Let's assume that the tree is, in fact, the person who drew it. In the drawing, it seems that the person is struggling with a difficult dilemma, facing the need to decide between staying at home, with the family, close to the mother, or going out into the world, to society, and coping with life.

The state of the tree indicates that it is already exhausted; it has no strength. It stands in place, not sprouting, not blooming. There is no life in it, only an endless struggle to survive.

This situation may leave the person unwilling to make a decision. They do not want to choose, so they stand still.

Perhaps they need to decide between the father's opinion and the mother's opinion. They want to please both.

How old is the person who drew it?

A child, an adolescent, or perhaps an adult?

Could it perhaps be a child of divorced parents, one who moves endlessly between father and mother, from the father's home to the mother's home?

On the face of it, it seems the struggle is still ongoing: with only one color tone, a brown representing being fixed to the earth. There are no optimistic colors of hope, not even black for darkness; no sky blue, no birds of change and hope for new plans; the tree is just standing in one place and struggling with the opposing forces being exerted on it.

Do you think it could be an adolescent wrestling with their sexual identity?

If so, why do you think so? What gives you that feeling?

DRAWING NO. 25: THE LONG NECK, WHY?

The first impression is that there is an adolescent with difficulty in expression; the adolescent seems under pressure.

Two things draw my attention: the squinting eyes and the narrow, long neck.

There are several possibilities. One is that the head is very small relative to the adolescent's body. The second possibility is that the neck is very large relative to the body. Each option carries a different meaning.

The eyes' squinting can have several causes. The first is a physical issue related to the eye muscles.

Another possibility is a fixed gaze at a certain point in front of the adolescent, or anxiety and fear, a desire to avoid something or someone looking at you.

Let's expand on the possibilities we mentioned.

The long neck and the head

As I noted in the chapter on figure drawing, the neck connects emotion, the heart, to the brain, the intellect.

Let's currently address the assumption that the head is very small relative to the body. The meaning here is the artist's diminishment of themselves and their intellectual abilities. A lack of faith in those abilities. This diminishment can open up many questions about why they feel this way. It could be related to the social group they are with, family, friends, or classmates. It could also be that they feel this way due to a lack of success in academic fields or games against friends.

If the neck is very large in the child's small body, then it is a hint related to the neck, difficulty with things connected to the neck, swallowing, for example, or inflammation; that is, on the physical level. On the emotional level, a very broad neck can tell us about a rapid link between heart and mind, a mixing of the two areas that may indicate confusion.

Regarding the eyes, I tend to assess that this is a focusing of the gaze on something very close to the nose, to the eyes. This happens when we are afraid of an insect approaching our nose.

If we summarize these points, it seems to me, based on the impressions and the signs, that we are looking at a combination of factors: a child who struggles both emotionally and cognitively, anxious about something approaching.

DRAWING NO. 26: THE CHILD ON THE ROOF

My initial feeling is that this is a family without a mother, or that the mother is absent from the home for long periods.

- Why is the child on the roof?
- Why is one figure inside the house, and the rest are outside?
- What is the message in the orange shirt, the color of the house?
- A connecting color?

The first thing we see at first glance in the drawing is, without a doubt, the child on the roof of the house. The first question that arises: why is the child on the roof?

There are many possible reasons: it could be part of a game, or it could be a desire to look far, to be seen from afar.

However, in my opinion, this is the wish and the need to be very close to the sun (the mother), within touching distance. But why only this child? What about the other children in the drawing? Why are they not turning toward the sun? Moreover, they are even "hidden" by the house, and one figure is inside the house. The connection with the mother (the sun) is the central focus; from here came my initial feeling that this is a family without a mother, or that the mother is absent from the home for long periods.

I continue with this hypothesis: it may be a family of a father and four children. The father is inside the house; three children are next to the house, and one is on the roof.

Why is there a figure inside the house and the rest outside?

Most likely, the figure inside the house is the father. He is busy with his own things, and also looks out the window and watches over the children playing outside. It is possible, if I try to link it to the central focus, that the mother is actually at home sick, which obligates the father to stay in the home.

We can also see that the color of his shirt is different from the children's blue; this is also true of the little child, about whom I will elaborate later.

The connection between the colors

In every drawing, or in the great majority of them, there is a wide range of colors. There is a term you will now learn: "linking colors." When we see several elements in the same color, as in this drawing, where the children's shirts are the same color, the drawer's aim, consciously or not, is to tell us: "There is a direct connection between these elements," in this case, the children.

In one of the drawings I encountered in the past, the subject was a sexual assault in a huge playground. The drawing was in a profusion of colors, almost paradise. But on a second look, and while interpreting the drawing, one could see the attacker, two victims, and the sun, all emphasized in the same color, a loud red. Red did appear in the drawing, but in other shades than that strident hue. Of course, there were additional signs, and together with those symbols with "the linking red," there was no doubt it was a sexual assault in the park.

What is the message in the orange shirt, the color of the house?

We see that the younger boy's shirt is the house's orange. The younger boy appears half-transparent, but the color of the pants is blue, identical to his siblings', and the head is in natural colors. If the younger boy drew the picture, he is saying: "I feel transparent, I feel unseen, but I am here!" If another sibling had drawn the picture, this message would look different; perhaps the entire child would be in a different color, or all of them would be in the color of the house.

There is also another possibility: perhaps the child on the roof is an adopted child who is looking for his biological mother. That is definitely a reasonable possibility, and it fits with the direction of the central line that touches the mother, which could also explain why all the other figures do not "make contact" with the mother.

These are the examples I chose to expand upon from the practice chapter. You are invited to choose any other drawing from the chapter, or even not from the chapter, and interpret it yourselves. You can upload your interpretation to the WhatsApp group. We will be able to discuss the drawing and its interpretation there together.

CLOSING REMARKS

This page is a summary of over twenty years of life and professional experience, distilled into four years of focus, formulation, and writing. The purpose of the process was to create for you a complete and comprehensive guide to interpreting drawings by children, adolescents, and families. By reading and doing the exercises in the book, each and every one of you has acquired a solid foundation that enables you to embark on your journey as professional, skilled drawing interpreters.

Parents, teachers, preschool teachers, social workers, and welfare professionals – you are now at an ideal starting point to become some of the best drawing interpreters.

Even after decades of experience and hands-on work with hundreds and thousands of drawings, the learning never ends: every day, new insights emerge; we keep reading, practicing, and discovering further worlds in the field.

I invite you to join my study group, to enjoy daily professional support, and take the opportunity to increase your motivation to deepen your knowledge and understanding.

Thank you very much for your support and partnership. See you on the path ahead.

Koby Avraham

WHAT IS HIDDEN BEHIND A LINE, COLOR, SYMBOLS, AND SIGNS IN A DRAWING?

The book before you opens a window into the vulnerable world of children, adolescents, and families, through a tool that is academically researched, simple, and marvelous: the interpretation of drawings by children, adolescents, and families.

Through practical examples, professional analyses, and clear language, you will learn how to identify emotions, distresses, dreams, and life experiences that are hidden among the symbols in the drawing, the pencil lines, and the shades on the page.

Koby Avraham, B.A. in Behavioral Sciences and M.A. in Social Change through the Arts, has over twenty years of experience in interpreting drawings by children and adolescents. He combines academic knowledge, work with families and professional teams, with personal experiences from his own childhood, experiences that shaped his mission to give children another voice, even when they struggle to speak.

The book also addresses the field of sensory system regulation and offers ways to understand how diverse sensory experiences are reflected in drawings and influence processes of expression, learning, and behavior.

A complete professional guide for parents, educators, therapists, social workers, and anyone who seeks to deepen their listening to what children are saying... without words.

A book that will open your eyes, spark curiosity, provide practical tools, and invite you to see and feel beyond the colors.

The Complete Professional Guide to Understanding the World of Children, Adolescents, and Families Through Drawings
Experienced, Tested, Learned, and Written by

Koby Avraham, M.A. in Social Change through the Arts

September 2025

www.ingramcontent.com/pod-product-compliance
Lightning Source LLC
LaVergne TN
LVHW052149210926
848482LV00019B/298
* 9 7 9 8 9 0 2 2 3 6 0 7 8 *